ROLLS-ROYCE
THE GROWTH OF A FIRM

By the same author

ROLLS-ROYCE: THE YEARS OF ENDEAVOUR
ROLLS-ROYCE: THE MERLIN AT WAR

THE FAVOURITE PORTRAIT OF CHARLES.
The Hon. C. S. Rolls

ROLLS-ROYCE

THE GROWTH OF A FIRM

IAN LLOYD

First published 1978 by
THE MACMILLAN PRESS LTD
London and Basingstoke
Associated companies in Delhi
Dublin Hong Kong Johannesburg Lagos
Melbourne New York Singapore Tokyo

British Library Cataloguing in Publication Data

Lloyd, Ian
Rolls-Royce, the growth of a firm
1. Rolls-Royce – History
2. Automobile industry and trade –
Great Britain – History
I. Title
338.7'62'922220941   HD9710.G74R5

ISBN 978-1-349-03913-5   ISBN 978-1-349-03911-1 (eBook)
DOI 10.1007/978-1-349-03911-1

To the memory of my mother,
who came of a generation that believed
in excellence and whose encouragement
never failed

Contents

List of Appendixes

List of Illustrations

Preface

The reader will feel entitled to some explanation of the reason for a delay of nearly thirty years between the writing and the eventual publication of a history of Rolls-Royce, of which this book forms the first part. *The Years of Endeavour* and *The Merlin at War* will eventually take the history to 1945 and form part of the original study which I completed at Cambridge in 1949.

This explanation is in itself an interesting story. When Ernest Hives (later Lord Hives, C.H.) gave his agreement to my undertaking this study as the central theme of the work for a postgraduate degree, I was allowed unfettered access to all Rolls-Royce papers and personnel on the clear understanding that subsequent publication would be a matter for discussion. This was a remarkably generous offer and presented a unique opportunity to a student of British industrial problems. The completed work, especially the section dealing with the Second World War which will appear in the third book, *The Merlin at War*, proved in the event to be much more controversial than I had anticipated or intended. My academic mentors at Cambridge were disturbed by the effect of some of my conclusions on the economic thinking current in the University at that time, for the University was not sympathetic towards this form of study, which was still comparatively novel and brought industry in an uncomfortable way within the ivory tower of 'pure' economics. News of this controversy, inevitably, reached Derby and is one reason why Hives was reluctant to permit publication.

Hindsight has since furnished a further explanation. The dependence of Rolls-Royce on the provision of government finance, and particularly of research and development support for the new generation of jet turbines then being developed for the civil and military markets, had not greatly diminished in the years immediately after the war. The relationship between the firm and the government of the day (the first post-war Labour Government of Mr Clement Attlee) was inevitably sensitive. Had this study been published at that time, with the apparent blessing of the board and management of Rolls-Royce, it could and almost certainly would have been misinterpreted as a polemic in favour of the free-enterprise system and an attack, by implication, on the central planning and control of aero-engine production in Great Britain. This reaction was never made explicit and is pure supposition on my part, but Hives gave no reasons and I was left to draw my own conclusions and honour my undertaking. All that was published at the time was a summary article entitled 'The Environment of Business Decision' in the *South African Journal of Economics*. This will be published as the final chapter of *The Merlin at War*.

It would be pointless to conceal the intense disappointment which I felt at the time, particularly as I believed that the political case for the free-enterprise system was not being put forward with the vigour and conviction which the situation in Britain demanded. Here was evidence which should be published and there was a clear and deep conflict between the requirements of academic freedom and the discharge of an obligation which I had accepted to obtain unfettered access to the relevant documents. It is easy to argue that it should never have been accepted, but I doubt whether in this or similar cases research students would ever be given such access without some obligation of this kind having to be accepted. But I assumed, at the time, that the restriction would be short-lived and turned my attention to another career in another country.

In 1971 the company whose history up to 1945 will be described in this and two succeeding books ceased to exist and I found myself involved as a Member of Parliament in the acrimonious debates in the House of Commons which surrounded the demise and subsequent nationalisation of a great British institution. All this may form part of another book which will take the history of the original Rolls-Royce company from 1945 to 1971 when, most regrettably and, in my view, unnecessarily, it ceased to exist. But that has yet to be written and while I remain in the House of Commons I am unlikely to find the time to write it. Everything which follows, with the exception of comparatively minor modifications of an editorial nature, was written before 1949 and the reader may occasionally have to remind himself that the conclusions reached and the judgements made were those which I made at the time.

The decision to publish was taken early in 1976. Since the old Rolls-Royce Company by then had ceased to exist, it seemed an appropriate time to enquire whether the original objections had fallen away. I approached Sir Kenneth Keith, Chairman of Rolls-Royce (1971) Ltd, the successor company, who generously agreed to publication. I should perhaps add that neither the present nor the former Rolls-Royce

Companies should be held responsible in any way for the views expressed, all of which were entirely my own. The history is the company's and it may now serve something of the wider purpose which I had in mind when it was originally written and which I attempted to describe in the remainder of the original preface, dated July 1949, which follows from this point onwards.

I.S.L.

September 1977

The history of a great industrial country is to a far larger extent than is generally realised the history of its great industrial enterprises. The lives of most people are more intimately affected by the success or failure of the individual organisation (under whatever general financial or political system that organisation operates) in all its various fields of endeavour than by the conspicuous and spectacular decisions of national or international politics. The survival of a country, both in peace and in war, can depend on the courage, initiative, foresight and imagination shown by management and employees even more than on the ability of its statesmen. That this should be so in war might seem obvious in the case of a firm like Rolls-Royce. It is less obvious, but no less true, in time of peace. The quality, intensity and direction of effort of all those who participate in an industrial undertaking is of vital importance to the survival not only of that undertaking but of the national and international economy of which it is part. But though this is generally recognised the few efforts which have been made to analyse and evaluate the complex factors which influence and determine the growth of a firm, the factors which determine the vitality of the social organisms which serve man's social and economic purposes, are hardly proportionate to the importance of the subject. The separate branches of the social sciences occasionally seek evidence from business records to prove or disprove theories conceived in theoretical isolation and developed with a pontifical disregard of the interaction of social, economic, political and personal forces in the large and complex environment of business decision. When reality is stretched too far upon the rack of theory, it is more often than not the rack which breaks.

This is an attempt to portray that environment in some detail, to analyse some of the lesser-known ingredients of success and failure, to give proper emphasis to the irrational and illogical elements in business growth, to personality and prejudice, to the importance of blind guesses and intuition as well as to careful calculation and the application of recognised techniques of industrial management. My purpose is to illustrate why so much of the economic theory relating to the firm which attempts to explain its functioning in terms of anything more precise than statements of general tendency succeeds only in distorting reality to a degree which makes its conclusions absurd and its prescriptions dangerous.

In his aptly titled book *The Magic of a Name*, Harold Nockolds has already written the story of some of the men who made Rolls-Royce and of the products which their ingenuity and persistence created. This book approaches the subject from a different angle. It is concerned more with the problem of growth and survival in the economic sense of a typical unit of a major British industry. For surprisingly enough Rolls-Royce is in many ways typical of the industry of which it forms a part. The history of the firm and of the industry cover roughly the same period, and the problems of the industry as a whole have been the problems of the firm. Rolls-Royce has had no special advantages and though it has created for itself an exceptional position by exceptional endeavour, it started in several respects less than equal with its competitors.

It is inevitably a study in leadership, of the real personality infused throughout the organisation from the beginning rather than the fictitious legal personage whose birth certificate was filed in Somerset House in 1906. It is the story of the struggle of a small handful of men with the social, political and financial forces which constitute the industrial environment of the early twentieth century, of their failure as well as their achievements. It is in large measure an attempt to analyse the contemporary impact of those forces which determine policy, and the extent to which the collective judgement of the organisation has responded to them.

Rolls-Royce is exceptional in its success as an economic organisation no less than for the technical quality of its products, and though the two are necessarily related they are not completely interdependent. From the economist's point of view this is of great interest. In the world of economic organisms there is no simple Darwinian law of survival, of adaptation or evolution. Yet survival is the result both of complex adaptation and progressive evolution, and the nature of economic adaptation and evolution, no less complex in a social or economic organisation than in a living species, is a subject about which very little is known. One reason for this is that the histories of the major industrial units of this and most other countries remain to be written. Cursory popular histories of some firms have been produced; more serious studies have been made of the evolution and structure of a number of major industries. But these are of necessity inadequate and incomplete if the detailed histories of the major component units are shrouded in a cloud of heroic and ineffectual secrecy, a legacy of the era when it was thought that success in a competitive society depended on divulging the absolute minimum of information about past achievement – or failure – and on the maximum misrepresentation of present intentions and activities.

As far as it has been possible for the management of Rolls-Royce to do so, this veil over the past has been lifted. The barriers which remain are those which harass the historian in any field – the loss or destruction of records and documents, the traditional and deep-seated attitudes of employees and others towards the outsider. Two world wars have brought about the destruction, both by enemy action and deliberate scrapping for salvage, of a great number of valuable records. Such a policy, eminently patriotic and sensible at the time, is one which the historian must inevitably condemn. For if an adequate insight is ever to be obtained into the functioning of economic and social forces, in a free-enterprise economy in particular, this will only be obtained by the constant testing of theoretical concepts and systems against the facts of economic growth and change. If these facts, when existent, are inaccessible, and when accessible are no longer extant, there can be little hope that theoretical models and formulations of economic forces will ever make any considerable approach towards explaining the historical reality of economic evolution.

In a review of Drucker's study of General Motors it was suggested by *The Economist* that there had yet to be written a study of industry which would do for industry what Lord Bryce's *American Commonwealth* did for the United States. Such a study would indeed make a vital contribution to the understanding and progress of industrial civilisation, but it is equally certain that the raw material for such a monumental analysis does not as yet exist, and its accumulation is beyond the power of any single individual. It is hoped that this study may make some small contribution to this future treatise, but it can be no greater than that of a mollusc to a coral reef. That it is made at all is due entirely to the broad-minded attitude of Rolls-Royce, who afforded the author every possible assistance.

Professor N.S.B. Gras concluded his introduction to the Harvard history of the House of Baring with the reflection that 'if British business firms and companies had written their histories and allowed scholars, journalists and politicians to learn what private business really involved, British history of the period following the Second World War would have been somewhat different. In Britain itself business history is still behind the iron curtain of the mythical entrepreneur'. This study is an attempt to lift an important section of that curtain. In making this possible Rolls-Royce has set an example which it is hoped will be widely followed. To the economist and the historian there lie open few more fascinating or instructive fields of research.

Sources and Acknowledgements

The main sources from which the information for this study has been obtained are the documents, memoranda, correspondence and minutes filed in the Rolls-Royce archives, to which I was given complete and unrestricted access through the courtesy of the then managing director, Mr Ernest W. Hives, and the board of directors. The only continuous record of policy is contained in the board minutes and the information contained in these twelve volumes varies greatly in quality and scope. During the early years of the company's history the discussions at board meetings seem to have been more fully recorded than in more recent times but unfortunately nearly all the supporting documents have not survived previously to 1937. This is partly because of the fact that the management in the early days was not interested in preserving a carefully documented record of the firm's activity and partly because a great deal of the material which did survive was destroyed in a paper salvage campaign during the Second World War. The 'archives' of the firm are archives in name only. The material was scattered geographically between Derby, London and Crewe and no central filing system existed. Few members of the management had any idea of what type of records existed and where they could be found. In many cases I was fortunate enough to discover important records which were thought to have been lost or destroyed. In this preliminary task of unearthing records I was particularly indebted to the sympathetic interest and patience of Mr R. B. Wilson, secretary of the company until 1948, Mr G. R. Strangeways, personal assistant to the managing director, Miss K. Wilkinson, Mr H. Grylls and Mr W. A. Robotham. The discovery of several important files of the early correspondence of Claude Johnson and Sir Henry Royce was due to the persistent searches carried out in the war-damaged cellars of the London headquarters of the company by Miss Crans.

The discovery of the valuable files of correspondence between Sir

Henry Royce and the engineering staff at Derby covering the periods of his absence at West Wittering and Le Canadel was quite accidental, as was the discovery of a large number of documents relating to the First World War, the negotiations in the United States and the formation of the first American subsidiary. For the opportunity to analyse this information I was greatly indebted to Mr F. C. **Champneys of Messrs Claremont Haynes, who produced for me six** tin trunks of legal documents in which had been filed copies of important policy papers of which no record whatever had survived in Rolls-Royce's own archives. I am also indebted to Mr Champneys for documents and details relating to the history of the Bentley Company.

Much of the material which made it possible for me to write a fairly detailed history of the Rolls-Royce Company at Springfield, Massachusetts, was obtained through the courtesy of Mr J. McManus, who had preserved several valuable documents and who made it possible for me to obtain the bankruptcy papers from the archives of the New York City legal department. Mr Henry J. Fuller, chairman of the American Rolls-Royce Company, afforded me the unusual privilege of reading his personal diaries covering his period of association with the Springfield plant and gave me a great deal of valuable information in a series of interviews. Further information on the American company was obtained from Mr L. J. Belnap, president of the Canadian Pulp and Paper Company of Montreal, and from the magnificent industrial library of the Society of Automobile Engineers in Detroit. Without this material it would not have been possible to obtain such a clear view of why Rolls-Royce decided to manufacture cars in the U.S.A., an important episode in the company's history which will be fully dealt with in *The Years of Endeavour*.

Arthur Gibbs, Basil Johnson, and Maurice Olley all produced most valuable records and information which I could not possibly have obtained in any other way. Mr Minchen, managing director of the National Battery Company, Mr Tildesley, Mr Evenden and Mr Wooler contributed interesting information on Sir Henry Royce's early work with the company. Mr R. S. Kellog, of the Marine Division of the Packard Motor Company, was instrumental in my obtaining all the information which I required on the production of the Packard Merlin in the United States. The chief archivist of the National Archives in Washington produced for me at very short notice the relevant papers of the Council for National Defense, the

Sources and Acknowledgements

American Embassy and several other bodies which were responsible for the American side of the negotiations on aero-engine production during the First World War. The corresponding archives in Great Britain for this period had not then been made generally available but Mr McNerney, senior historian of the Air Ministry Historical Department, produced several document which I might not otherwise have seen and made available to me parts of his own unpublished work on aero-engine production in the First World War.

Mr W. Clarke, the chief accountant, and Mr T. Easton responded magnificently to my requests for obscure and forgotten financial information of all kinds. Mr Pope, of the shipping department, produced for me the most complete and authentic figures on aero-engine production which I could discover. Mr T. Stoddardt and Mr S. E. Blackstone of Production Engineering Ltd provided reports and information relating to their period of association with Rolls-Royce during the Second World War. Major Bulman, of the Ministry of Supply, gave me valuable information on the rearmament period.

Had I endeavoured to list in detail the documents and correspondence from which most of the information used in this study has been obtained, the work would still be uncompleted and since the vast majority of the material is not generally available even to members of the company, there seemed little point in expanding an already substantial volume with numerous footnotes giving detailed references to particular letters, reports and memoranda. Apart from the material available in the archives of Rolls-Royce, however, I have made extensive use of the following sources:

M. Buist, *Rolls-Royce Memories* (Rolls-Royce; private printing)
Sir Winston Churchill, *The Second World War* (Cassell, 1948–52)
E. Devons, *Planning in Practice* (Cambridge University Press, 1950)
D. Eisenhower, *Crusade in Europe* (Heinemann, 1949)
Sir Roy Fedden, 'Report on a Mission to the United States in 1943' (unpublished)
Sir O. Franks, *Central Planning and Control in War and Peace* (London School of Economics, 1947)
J. Jewkes, *Ordeal by Planning* (Macmillan, 1948)
T. Lilley et al., *Problems of Accelerating Aircraft Production during World War II* (Bailey Bros, 1952)
T. Lilley and L. L. Horton, *Future Financial Problems of Conversion in the Aircraft Industry* (Harvard University Press)

E. Mayo and G. F. Lombard, *Teamwork and Labour Turnover in the Aircraft Industry of South California* (Harvard University Press)

Ministry of Munitions, *History of the Ministry of Munitions*, 12 vols. (HMSO, 1918–22)

Monographs on: Aero-engine Production
                Development and Design in the British Aircraft Industry
                The Evolution of the Jet Engine
                The Production of Tanks
                Quality in Aircraft Production
                Quantity in Aircraft Production
                (All prepared as background papers for the Official History of the Second World War, and not published in the form made available to the author.)

H. Nockolds, *The Magic of a Name* (G. T. Foulis & Co., 1939)

Sir Max Pemberton, *The Life of Sir Henry Royce* (1933)

Sir W. Raleigh and H. A. Jones, *The War in the Air*, 6 vols. (Oxford University Press, 1922–37)

R. Schlaifer and S. D. Heron, *The Development of Aircraft Engines and Fuels* (Bailey Bros, 1952)

T. Wilson, *Programmes and Allocations in the Planned Economy* (Oxford University Press, 1949)

The above list is by no means exhaustive. Several items of general information have been obtained from a number of volumes of press cuttings covering the inter-war years which fortunately survived the general devastation of Rolls-Royce's salvage campaign.

I was fortunate in being able to discuss many aspects of the company's history with innumerable members of the staff during the course of visits to Derby, Crewe, Barnoldswick, Glasgow and Hucknall. Though it is impossible to mention them all by name my indebtedness to them all is no less great for the fact of my not being able to do so. All gave freely of their time, their enthusiasm and their memories.

During the first year that I was engaged on this work at Cambridge Professor E. A. G. Robinson suggested many profitable avenues of exploration. Professor M. M. Postan encouraged and guided my labours throughout and made many valuable criticisms. In the final revision of this book for publication, I have had an opportunity to reconsider and, in many places incorporate some extremely valuable comments which were made, in a long letter to me in June 1952 by Philip W. S. Andrews, then a Fellow of Nuffield College, Oxford, who read the whole text with great care and whose strong encouragement and support at a most difficult time I remember with gratitude and affection. His early death deprived the then embryonic world of the business historian of a great pioneer, an economist whose feet were planted firmly on the ground of industrial reality.

My indebtedness to the board, the then managing director, Ernest Hives (later Lord Hives), and innumerable members of the staff of the Rolls-Royce Company is very great. From all I received every possible co-operation and assistance. It was a pleasure and a privilege to meet and work with them. From this and from many other points of view few economic historians could have been more fortunate in their choice of subject.

Lord Hives had generously suggested that I should read every document which I thought relevant to the subject and that I should allow no bias in the firm's favour to enter my selection of facts or choice of topics. I fulfilled this obligation as far as it was within my power to do so. No attempt was made to withhold any documents or information from me or to influence in any way the facts which I selected or the opinions which I expressed. The responsibility for both is entirely mine. I will confess, however, in retrospect, that this complete freedom has probably been quite the most effective method which the management could possibly have used to ensure the development of a subtle and responsible discretion. But though I have been conscious of its growth I have endeavoured to limit its influence and if the record set out in the following pages appears to offer little ammunition either to the zealous reformers of the private enterprise system or to the great host of its critics, who know so much about forestry and so little about trees, they must not attribute this too completely to the reinforcement of the slight predisposition with which I commenced this study. The record of this firm needed no bias to make it presentable to the outside world.

1 The Early Background

A great society is a society in which its men of business think greatly
of their functions.

Alfred North Whitehead

The history of Rolls-Royce lends itself readily to a chronological
division into eight periods, all of which are distinguished by particular
developments, problems and personalities. The first begins before the
turn of the century and continues to the actual foundation of the
company in 1906. The second brings the company through its formative
years to the outbreak of the First World War which it entered with a
strong reputation in the special field which it had done so much to
create, but otherwise completely unprepared for the remarkable part
which it was to play in that war and unaware of the extensive changes in
its organisation and activities which the war was to bring about.

These two periods form the subject-matter of this book, which takes
the company's history to the end of the First World War and the acute
problems created by disarmament. The third period ends with the
completion of reconversion in the early twenties and merges almost
imperceptibly after a series of crises and experiments into the fourth, the
decade which ended rather less abruptly in 1935 when the start of the
rearmament programme introduced a substantial and significant change
in the economic environment. The fifth, the period of rearmament,
ended with the outbreak of war in 1939 and the complete mobilisation of
the technical and administrative organisation which had been built up,
as much on the initiative of the firm itself as on that of the state, when it
was clear that war could not be avoided. The third, fourth and fifth
periods form the subject of the second part of the study, *The Years of
Endeavour*. The Second World War, in which Rolls-Royce played a most
conspicuous part as armourer to the R.A.F., forms the subject of the third
book to be published in this series under the title, *The Merlin at War*.

Each of these periods has a distinct character which will emerge as the
study proceeds, but the first period is dominated by the personality of
three men, a common personality almost, which the company has

1

acquired and developed. For a fictitious person that exists only in the eyes of the law Rolls-Royce has always manifested to a remarkable degree some of the personal characteristics of its founders. These characteristics have, without any conscious policy, become incorporated in an unwritten tradition which is followed, perhaps equally unconsciously, by most of its employees, and this is immediately perceptible to the outsider who meets them in any capacity. Most organisations probably reflect to some degree or other in their internal structure and inter-employee attitudes the character of their founders, but in this case it has been so marked that to begin this study with the immediate preliminaries leading to the formation of a public company in 1906 would present a most misleading picture.

It would also enhance the belief, already so prevalent, that economic organisations result from the interaction of purely impersonal forces and that individuals as such play very little part in the course of events. Had C.S. Rolls, F.H. Royce and Claude Johnson never lived, other engineering firms would doubtless have developed and produced excellent cars and aero-engines. The tradition of craftsmanship of the highest order in the mechanical world, which the endeavours of Rolls-Royce have done so much to establish, would no doubt have been developed by others. But Rolls-Royce, by any other name, would probably have followed a comparatively prosaic and mundane career.

F.H. Royce was himself a product of natural inborn ingenuity and determination, and of a harsh, but stimulating, environment. Born in 1863 at Alwalton, near Peterborough, the youngest of a large family, he was forced by the death of his father to fend for himself at an early age, after just over a year at an elementary school. It would be interesting to know just how many distinguished men have started life as newsboys and reached positions of eminence despite, or possibly because of, not having had a strictly conventional education. Royce was a product of this typically Victorian tradition, working as a newsboy for W.H. Smith and Son, in 1874, followed by another brief year at school, then a year as a telegraph boy for a London post office. This was followed by three rather more constructive and interesting years as an apprentice in the Great Northern Railway works at Peterborough, where he worked on locomotive engines. In this he was doubly fortunate, for one of the greatest of all British locomotive engineers, Patrick Stirling, was designing and building at Peterborough at this time, and the influence of his craftsmanship and personality may be judged from the fact that both Royce and Stroudley, another eminent locomotive engineer, were apprenticed at the Peterborough works under Stirling's reign. He also had the good fortune at Peterborough to work directly under an enthusiast, always one of the strongest influences, a Mr Yarrow, who had a home workshop and took a great interest in the young Royce. This phase of his career lasted long enough to ensure that Royce would continue his engineering training, and when financial stringency forced his aunt to terminate his apprenticeship, he went to Leeds and obtained work in a machine tool firm where he was paid 11/- a week for a 54-hour week. 'Part of this time,' he says[1] '– for months – I had to work from 6 a.m. to 10 p.m. and all Friday night.' This did not last long, and Royce decided that London offered better opportunities. Here he obtained work with the Electric Light and Power Co., a pioneer in its field, where he acquired a specialised knowledge of the new technology of electricity both from practical work which he did for the company and also by attending the Finsbury Polytechnic night-classes where he studied under a Professor Ayrton. Electricity was then a very novel phenomenon, and regarded very sceptically by industrialists. Although Royce perceived its possibilities and was one of the first in the field, he had the misfortune to be associated with a concern which was unable to offer him any real continuity of occupation. Soon after arriving in Liverpool on promotion to the position of chief electrician to the Electrical Company, a branch of the London company, the latter went into liquidation and he was once more thrown on his own resources.[2]

While still employed by the Electrical Company Royce had met a young man by the name of Claremont, who later became the first chairman of the Rolls-Royce board, and they decided in 1884 to establish their own firm to manufacture electrical appliances. Operations started in a very modest way in Cooke Street, Manchester, with a capital of £75. The principal products of this concern were electric bell sets, lampholders, switches, fuses, and registering instruments. The firm prospered and Royce subsequently turned his attention to dynamos, switchboards and electric cranes. In a letter to Claude Johnson he has described his work at this time.

In dynamo work, in spite of insufficient ordinary and technical education I managed to conceive the importance of sparkless commutation, the superiority of the drum-wound armature for continuous current dynamos, and Royce Ltd. of Manchester was famous for continuous current dynamos which had sparkless commutation in the days before carbon brushes. . . .

While at Liverpool in 1882/3 I conceived the value of a 3 wire system of conductor in efficiency and economy of distribution of electricity and also afterwards the scheme of maintaining a constant potential at a distant point. Both of these I successfully applied.

Royce rapidly established a reputation for his dynamos in the Midlands, where there was a growing demand for them in woollen and cotton mills. The firm prospered sufficiently for the two partners to marry two sisters in 1893, a venture which incidentally brought a further £1500 of capital into the business. In the following year F.H. Royce Ltd. was established as a limited company, and the future seemed reasonably assured, though there was at this time according to Royce 'severe foreign competition in dynamos and motors'. On two occasions disaster was very narrowly averted. Royce had just installed a large motor in the cotton mill of an important customer when it was discovered by Claremont that it was making a most unusual noise. Unobtrusive inspection revealed that this was due to creep of the armature and that it might fail at any time. This meant that it would have to be replaced, involving a suspension of operations throughout the mill for several days. The millowner confirmed this suspicion, and Royce immediately suggested that in view of his great dependence on the motor, there should be a spare armature. The millowner agreed and Royce worked all night, a by no means unusual occurrence, to produce a spare. This of course had to be installed in the motor to be tested, and having once done this Royce suggested that there was no point in stopping the mill a third time to replace the original. The millowner readily agreed to this, and the defective armature lay at the side of the motor for its entire life. The 'spare' did not fail. The second disaster was narrowly averted by the acumen of the secretary, a young man by the name of De Looze (later secretary of Rolls-Royce) who insisted on insuring a large number of orders which Royce had just installed in another cotton mill. At the insurance office something prompted him to tell the clerk to put the time on the cover note, which he did. The inevitable happened. The mill was gutted by fire that evening, and the insurance paid out in full. These may appear somewhat trivial incidents in the history of a great company, but they are examples of that thoroughness and ingenuity in both technical and commercial matters which weights the scales of fortune on the side of success.

Royce next turned his attention to electric cranes which he did a great deal to develop. He took out the first basic patent for a governor device which limited the downward speed of a crane. This work arose from his horror of accidents, particularly in steelworks, where some of the cranes which he had installed had to carry crucibles of molten metal. The firm also equipped a number of shipbuilding yards and Royce cranes achieved a reputation for quality and reliability. All were fitted with roller bearings which Royce manufactured himself as they could not be obtained elsewhere. He was asked to manufacture motors for canal lock-gates and in building these developed a worm gear of a type then little known. In their construction he employed the technique of gear-shaving, this being the first recorded instance of its use. Thus, by the turn of the century, he had acquired a thorough and varied experience in several important fields of engineering. More important possibly than the knowledge of existing engineering techniques thus obtained was the fact that he had developed the ability to create new techniques and to solve problems in relatively novel fields. His real genius lay in development work. There was nothing which he could not improve and few mechanical devices which he did not want to improve or succeed in improving.

When Royce bought his first powered vehicle, a French Decauville,[3] there was no real motor industry in Great Britain, and even in France the most famous cars were the product of small workshops and enthusiastic amateurs.[4] They were regarded by the general public either as a novelty or as a menace, at best a contraption which offered to those who were mechanically minded a constant source of entertainment, and offended the eye, ear, and dignity of those who were not. The law was strongly biased in favour of the pedestrian, who considered that the motor-car had a legal obligation to avoid him, even under the most absurd conditions. In 1905 the Marquess of Queensberry, serious in demeanour if not in intention, made an application to a London magistrate to keep a gun 'to shoot motorists who endanger the lives of himself and his family'. In August 1905 a Mr E.A. Macdonald was summoned on a charge 'That he did use on the Highway, to wit, Regent Street, a locomotive then in charge of one, George Candy, which did not consume, as far as practicable, its own smoke'.

The fact that the value of cars imported into England increased, according to the estimate of a motor journal, from £806,000 in 1903 to £1,448,000 in 1906 was considered to be proof of the 'spending power of the upper classes in what are called bad times'.[5]

The French motor industry seems to have set the pattern for the British which was making strenuous efforts to establish itself. The average firm in both countries produced a few hundred cars a year, and literally almost as many models as it produced cars. The customer generally ordered his chassis, engine and body work to be made to his own tastes. Many cars ostensibly manufactured in England were made entirely from French parts, and a good deal of British capital was invested either directly in French companies producing in France, or in British companies set up to produce the same model in England. Early in 1906 S. F. Edge, one of the pioneers of the British motor industry, started a violent controversy on the question of whether the value of British manufactured cars exceeded the value of imports. The figures which he obtained from manufacturers to prove his case reveal that out of 42 so-called manufacturers, only six produced more than 25 cars a week.[6] and all the remainder produced less than ten. At the 1906 Paris Show eighty-two French manufacturers exhibited. There was some justification for the observation made by H. Sturmey in a paper read before the Automobile Club on 18 December 1904 that 'little firms with an odd £1,000 or so capital filled themselves up with foreign goods to the immense benefit of continental manufacturers, and then finding the public did not scramble for their goods, had a scramble amongst themselves to get quit of them.'[7] Sturmey considered that it took the best part of two years to organise a factory to produce a satisfactory car but this did not deter a good number of people (who had reasonable workshops and thought that they knew better) from attempting to produce a car. In November 1906, just before Rolls-Royce's first public issue, the editor of the *Motor Trader* attributed the relative backwardness of the British motor industry to other causes.

> For the most part of ten years the British motor industry has been swinging on an ebb tide. It is generally agreed that one of the chief factors in prolonging the period of suspense and trial has been the disinclination of the British capitalist or inventor to put money into the British motor industry.

If the British capitalist did exhibit this disinclination, and it seems that the comment is justified, it was certainly not for lack of opportunity. But a good number of appeals for funds were based on little more than optimism, and the investor's reluctance is not altogether surprising. Royce pursued a more successful course, more by accident than design. He considered his Decauville to be a brilliant achievement completely marred by careless workmanship. (The flywheel of this car was held on by a taper-ended setscrew.) He admired French cars and maintained that they were the first vehicles to be properly designed for the purpose. He showed no interest in American cars, whose engineering he regarded as primitive. Having a little time on his hands, Royce set out to remedy the deficiencies of the Latin engineering temperament which his Decauville exhibited in so glaring a fashion.

He definitely did not set out with the idea of making a complete car, and at this stage, had no intention whatever of manufacturing one. But in bringing the Decauville up to his own high standards he virtually redesigned the whole car and eventually produced a completely different and, in a number of important aspects, superior product.[8]

Late in 1903 Royce had begun work on the construction of a two-cylinder 10 h.p. car and from the very beginning he concentrated on those qualities which are the indices of efficiency in any engineering product – silence, lightness, durability and reliability. With two young apprentices, Haldenby and Platford, both of whom were to feature prominently in the later history of Rolls-Royce, he worked steadily and unremittingly on the car, which many of the others thought a wild and expensive venture that monopolised his time and ability to the detriment of other engineering work. As it was, Royce worked an excessively long day and an even longer week, his idea of a restful weekend being to take home one of the experimental chassis to see if he could break anything on it or induce it to misbehave. He expected others to work with him, and though long hours were not regarded in quite the same light as they are today it is a tribute to the personality of the man that they invariably did so without complaint. The industrial system seems to create two types of 'slave'. The one submits to the slavery of routine with a reluctance which never really disappears, and the other becomes a devotee to his work, his entire life completely subordinated to the demands of his fanaticism.[9] To the latter the material reward is of no major significance. Royce became a slave to the idea of mechanical perfection in the particular manifestation of the internal combustion engine and the vehicle which carried it. Such men are not principally motivated by economic considerations, and they frequently induce others to share their fanaticism and dedication. Such methods are successful, but often costly in human terms and it was Royce himself who eventually paid the highest price.

The first 'Royce' car ran on 1 April 1904, and was a complete success. Only three examples of this, the 10 h.p. model, were ever made, but they established an immediate reputation. One was sold to Claremont,

1. The 10 h.p. Royce, the first car built by Henry Royce

Royce's partner, who was also a fellow director of Henry Edmunds on the Royce Board and on the Board of a firm of cable makers, W. T. Glover & Co., Ltd. Edmunds, in addition to being a member of the Automobile Club Committee, was a friend of C. S. Rolls and Claude Johnson, then running an agency in London for several prominent makes of French car. Edmunds sent a photograph and specifications of the 'Royce' to an initially unenthusiastic Rolls.[10] Royce refused to go to London and finally Rolls and Edmunds journeyed north to Manchester in the first week of May 1904. Royce was apparently not so much influenced by the commercial possibilities of actually manufacturing and selling this car as by the personal convenience to himself and his friends of being able to save time by using a reliable vehicle. None of the Royce cars had yet been offered to the public or advertised, and it was only Rolls's enthusiasm which induced Edmunds to arrange for him to meet Royce, which he did within three weeks of the first appearance of the car on the road.

This almost casual association was rapidly fused by an identity of interest as close as their past backgrounds, apart from a common interest in the motor-car, had been divergent. The Hon. C. S. Rolls was the third son of Lord Llangattock. Educated at Eton and Trinity College, Cambridge, where he took a first in Mechanics and Applied Science, he established a considerable reputation for himself by owning, in Cambridge, the first car ever to grace the precincts of an institution which has not always welcomed the noisy and disturbing products of mechanical progress. Rolls's interest, first in cars and then in aeroplanes, was to occupy very fully the short but adventurous career which he devoted almost entirely to exploiting the possibilities of the car, which the public considered dangerous, and the aeroplane, which the public found difficult to believe.

By the time he met Royce, Rolls had established a successful and well-known car agency and had enlisted the aid of a businessman of unusual ability, Claude Johnson. Both were good businessmen, both were publicists of the first order. Rolls took part as a racing driver in all the important events, and established a reputation as a gallant and daring driver. A car which received his recommendation was fortunate, and Rolls seemed to be prepared to sell the cars that he drove, rather than drive the cars which he sold. Claude Johnson was the human catalyst who fused the genius of Royce and the infectious enthusiasm of Rolls. There is no doubt that Rolls-Royce would not have attained the pre-eminent position which it holds today had it not been for the inspired leadership, initiative and enterprise of this unusual man, who regarded himself purely as a businessman of mediocre ability. But it was Johnson, more than either Rolls or Royce, who, at this point in its development, cast the destiny of the enterprise which came to be known as Rolls-Royce in the mould of greatness.

Claude Johnson had a career as unconventional as that of Royce. His father was a distinguished curator of the South Kensington museum, who had made a considerable personal sacrifice to give his large family a good education. Claude was sent to St Pauls, and went from there to the South Kensington art school where he succeeded only in convincing himself that he could not draw, and Sir Philip Cunliffe-Owen that his talents were considerable in other directions. He left the art school to become an organiser of exhibitions for various government departments and other bodies, and rapidly established a reputation for himself in a field which both required and developed a high degree of organising and administrative ability. His interest in the motor-car was attracted at first by the French cars which began to make their appearance in 1896 when Panhard-Levassor, De Dion, Daimler, Peugeot and Serpollet were becoming household words. But the Napier, Lanchester, Wolseley and several other British makes soon appeared, and Johnson was asked to

2. The 10 h.p. Royce chassis

3. The 10 h.p. Royce engine

organise an exhibition at the Imperial Institute. This gave him many contacts throughout the small but enthusiastic field of men interested in the industry, and F. R. Simms and Harrington Moore suggested to him that he should join in the foundation of the Royal Automobile Club. This he did with great energy, and he eventually became the first secretary of that organisation.

Thus when the 'Royce' first set its wheels upon the road, both Rolls and Johnson had already developed a considerable knowledge of the industry. After he had seen the 'Royce', Rolls confided to Edmunds in a letter that it was his ambition to see a really first-class British car produced, 'a good high-class quality car to replace the Panhard, preferably of three or four cylinders'. At the meeting in Manchester Royce agreed to manufacture for Rolls, who became his sole agent. The output of the Manchester shop was far too small for Rolls to be able to give up his other agencies, but it seems that Rolls contemplated doing so as soon as possible, for the 1904 agreement required Royce to design and manufacture four different chassis of 10, 15, 20 and 30 h.p. In November 1904 C. S. Rolls & Co. advertised that they were introducing an all-British car as part of their 'extensive programme' for 1905, and that this car would be on view for the first time at the Paris Show. Not only was the 10 h.p. car exhibited at the Show, but a 15 h.p. chassis, a 20 h.p. car and a 30 h.p. engine also made their appearance. Royce had been wasting no time. All received high praise from the technical press. It is interesting to notice that the 10 h.p. was never sold as the 'Royce', but as the Rolls-Royce. The name was mentioned for the first time in one of C. S. Rolls & Co.'s advertisements in the *Autocar* in December 1904 which described the 'first simple, silent Rolls-Royce'.[11] The Rolls-Royce Company was not formed for more than another year, but a distributing agency operating directly under the control of C. S. Rolls & Co. was registered under the name of Rolls-Royce Distributing Co. Ltd. This was a purely formal arrangement. Royce Ltd continued its separate existence in Manchester, though Royce now devoted most of his time to the design and production of cars. C. S. Rolls & Co. also retained its separate identity, and Rolls considered that it would be unwise because of the goodwill value of his name to attempt to alter it for some time. Rolls continued to sell other cars, principally the Minerva, Orleans and Panhard Levassor, but the Rolls-Royce occupied an increasingly large proportion of his advertising space, and, what is more important, of his advertising energy. The 20 h.p. car which had been named the 'Grey Ghost' was standardised, and the two- and three-cylinder cars were

4. The first 6-cylinder 30 h.p. Rolls-Royce Pullman Limousine exhibited at Olympia in 1905

dropped, an intelligent and courageous step. The object was to develop this type of car as a competitor for the first Tourist Trophy race to be held that year (1905) in the Isle of Man.

Lack of standardisation was already becoming a serious problem for the industry. Very few firms enjoyed a seller's market for their products, and those which did not do so attributed the success of those which did to the range of models which they produced to cater for all tastes and pockets. The Gladiator Company advertised the fact that 'No Gladiator car is finished or assembled before a definite order for same has been received thus leaving the individual purchaser a certain limit to indulge in his fancies regarding ignition, outfit, etc.' In a strong editorial the *Motor Trader* condemned what it considered to be 'scarcely sufficient commercialism and too much experimentalism' resulting from manufacturers 'endeavouring to spread themselves over too much ground. They want to supply any order which reaches them whether it be for an 8 h.p. single-cylinder car or a 60 h.p. six-cylinder. In the multitude of pattern there is no profit.'

The warning was heeded by few, and was eventually disregarded even by Rolls-Royce itself many years later. It was not pursued thoroughly

5. The Legalimit V-8

even by Royce for some time, and in 1905 and 1906 he continued to manufacture several distinct types including an extraordinary eight cylinder, constant-speed V-8 type known as the Legalimit. This car was not a success and few were produced. This policy was probably due to the insistent demands which Rolls was making for more and more cars of any type as long as they were made by Royce Ltd. Moreover financial, as well as technical, competition was an ever-present danger and both Daimler and Panhard announced considerable price reductions towards the end of 1905.

Rolls and Johnson were meanwhile establishing the name of the car both by competing with it in all the important endurance, long-distance, reliability and Tourist Trophy competitions, and by placing the car at the disposal of the press whenever occasion offered. Misfortune robbed Rolls of first place in the first Isle of Man TT in 1905, but P. C. Northey brought his car in second against considerably higher-powered competitors. Favourable comment was almost universal and owners began to write enthusiastic letters to the motor press extolling the virtues of their cars. At the end of the year orders were greatly in excess of the capacity of the works and Rolls gained considerable publicity by announcing at a trade dinner that he would in future trade only in British cars and fit British accessories wherever possible. Amalgamation of the two legal entities which were in fact the same firm was an obvious step, and Rolls-Royce Ltd was formally registered at Somerset House on 15 March 1906 with a nominal capital of £60,000. The new company did not in fact take over the entire activities of Royce Ltd. It took over the whole of the business and assets of C. S. Rolls & Co. and the motor side of Royce Ltd, which continued as a completely separate company until it was wound up in the thirties after its founder's death. Since a new factory was obviously required, Royce and Johnson planned to build one almost immediately. Most of the rest of the year 1906 was spent in arranging the details of the transaction and in making arrangements for the first public issue, which took place in December. The publicity side was not neglected and Rolls won the 1906 TT and followed this up by a magnificent performance at Ormond Beach, Florida, where he was beaten only by a Mercedes of more than twice the horsepower. The 6-cylinder 20 h.p. which he used on both occasions was first introduced to the public in September 1905 and was such a success that on 12 May 1906 there appeared for the first time an advertisement stating that the six-cylinder Rolls-Royce was 'Not one of the best – the Best in the World.' The superlative in advertising was used with some justification less than three years after the first two-cylinder car had been driven out of the Manchester works. Such an advertisement was by no means exceptional at this time. Many different concerns employed almost identical phrases and exaggerated claims were common; but Rolls-Royce seemed able to fulfil the great expectations which such advertisements caused, and throughout the company's history the reputation established by its earliest products proved a stern taskmaster.

Both Rolls Ltd and Royce Ltd were small and reasonably prosperous firms and it might be thought that, having proved the car, their amalgamation and entrance into the motor industry proper was a logical and simple step. It may indeed have been logical, but it was nevertheless a bold move considering the general state of the motor industry at this time. Competition was fierce, and there had been a boom in motor and omnibus flotations during the previous two years. The City was justifiably wary of motor company shares after two or three large omnibus 'reconstructions' had taken place, and the mortality rate in the industry was very high. Every new motor venture was looked upon with a critical eye and Rolls-Royce Ltd was no exception. But if the experts, as is so often the case, were wrong over Rolls-Royce the record of the industry was far from encouraging. The Argyll Motor Co. was floated in 1905 and an issue of £232,000 was heavily oversubscribed. This company erected a palatial factory at Alexandria in Scotland and drew the comment that 'with the amount of capital they had they would be able to put down works of such magnitude and with such appliances that they would be placed in a position to absolutely defy competition.' The works were erected and excited the admiration of the press and the motoring world, but competition was not defied. The company was liquidated and reorganised in 1908. In November 1904 Daimler had been reconstructed on the basis of a new issue of £200,000. Nine types of car were to be replaced by one. Humber, which had likewise raised a large amount of capital to equip a new works, also announced a policy of one standardised design.

Flotations of motor and omnibus companies in the year 1906 amounted to £3.7 million of which more than half was raised for the manufacture of cars. In May, the figure was just over a million pounds. Only a small number of the companies floated in this boom year survived, yet it is a characteristic of the boom that most businessmen allowed their better judgement to be swayed by the prevailing optimism, and Rolls, Royce and Johnson were no exceptions. Though *The Economist* was warning its readers against the spate of flotations and drawing revealing comparisons with the preceding motor-cycle boom, they decided to disregard the sceptical attitude of an elderly and respectable age towards the contraption which it regarded as the vehicle only of the youthful and adventuresome, and to proceed with a public issue for the purpose of building and equipping a new factory. Their existing financial resources were slender.

C. S. Rolls Ltd, whose first premises were at Lillie Hall in London, had been sufficiently impressed by trade prospects to lease a showroom in Conduit Street, where the company has remained to the present day. The balance sheet on 30 June 1906 reveals that there was a fairly substantial overdraft, and although a large amount of the firm's resources were tied up in the stock of cars, the overall financial position was fairly strong. From this it was estimated that the real assets of the company exclusive of goodwill amounted to £15,000. Though the goodwill was obviously of some considerable value, there was obviously no possibility of C. S. Rolls & Co. making any considerable contribution to the cost of floating a new company and equipping a new factory. Unfortunately no balance sheet of Royce Ltd has survived, but it is clear from the agreement that Royce Ltd was only disposing of its motor manufacturing shops and of the skill of Royce himself. The former it was able to replace, the latter it was not, and Royce, who devoted the greater part of his energies to the design of cars and engines for the rest of his life, had to return periodically to the old company to solve its problems and keep it going. It was finally wound up just after the great depression.

The first mention of a scheme to wind up the distributing company and establish the newly registered company on a firm basis appears in a letter from Ernest Claremont to his brother Albert, who became legal adviser to the new company, a position still held by the firm of Claremont Haynes. In this letter he refers to the options of Messrs Lazenby Bros and a Mr Steveacre on a scheme apparently drawn up some months before. They thought it unsound and Ernest Claremont concluded that Rolls-Royce should be less ambitious and start off in a smaller way.

About this time a series of interesting estimates was made of what the production costs of the new company would be on the basis of three possible figures for chassis output. These indicate that no really thorough estimates were made. They are little more than broad guesses intended to give those responsible a rough idea of the amount of capital and working capital they were likely to need. They may be profitably compared with the type of estimate which was made forty years later.

More accurate or detailed estimates may of course have been made, but they have not survived. These figures[12] reveal several interesting points:

(1) There was a clear intention to increase chassis output considerably. Only 60 chassis were produced in 1905.
(2) No allowance is made for any item of cost varying to any extent with increase in output.
(3) The calculation of 'men per acre' is rather crude, but seems to have been often used at this time.
(4) No attempt is made to separate overheads and direct costs.

The original capital of £60,000 was divided up into £33,000 preference, £22,000 ordinary and £5000 deferred shares of £1 each. Of this total only £17,009 preference, 22,000 ordinary and the whole 5000 deferred shares were allotted. In addition debentures to the value of £8500 were issued to Royce Ltd in return for certain tools and equipment already taken over solely for the manufacture of cars. C. S. Rolls Ltd held 10,000 of the preference shares and the 5000 deferred, which were later converted to ordinary; and Royce Ltd 7000 preference and all the ordinary. The 5000 deferred shares were first issued to Royce Ltd and transferred on 15 May 1906 to C. S. Rolls, but the reasons for this transaction are not known.

On 6 November the board decided to increase the capital to £200,000 and to issue £100,000 to the public immediately. Authority was given to underwrite the issue, but it was decided to proceed whether or not the backing of underwriters was obtained. At the same meeting authority was given to the secretary, De Looze, to request a land surveyor by the name of Ogden to 'ascertain general particulars of sites about 4 acres in extent off the Stretford Road between these works and Longford Bridge, and give us his general opinion of the relative merits of any one of such sites.' The general intention at this stage seems to have been to erect the new works near the old in Manchester. On 11 December it was formally resolved to take over C. S. Rolls Ltd for 14,434 preferred and 12,000 £1 ordinary shares, and to take over Rolls-Royce Distributing Ltd for £1000 in cash and to wind it up. At this meeting of the board a Mr A. H. Briggs was elected a director. Briggs, a man of considerable wealth, was a great Rolls-Royce enthusiast and his election to the board proved to be a farsighted move.

In preparing the estimates of future profits for the prospectus the published balance sheets of at least two other motor manufacturing companies were carefully considered. These two were Daimlers and Argylls. The former was registered in 1904 with a capital of £200,000 of which £142,568 had been issued, and had been outstandingly successful in 1905 and 1906. The profit in 1905 was £83,167, 57 per cent on invested capital, and in 1906 it increased to £213,469, 110 per cent on invested capital. Argylls, which had been registered in 1904 to acquire the business of the Hozier Engineering Company for the purpose of car manufacture, had made a considerably less spectacular profit of £26,633, 10.6 per cent on a paid-up capital of £244,904, in 1905 and 13.1 per cent in the following year. Argyll Motors made a further issue to the public of £100,000 on 8 December, one week before the Rolls-Royce issue.

Early in November, Claude Johnson wrote to Claremont, the chairman, discussing the prospects of the issue.

We cannot [he said] have a better time to go before the public than the present when they are made greedy by the announcement of the extraordinary profits of the Daimler Company.

He went on to discuss the names that appear on the board in the prospectus and remarked that

> An investor would not feel any confidence in the affair because Rolls's
> name is on it, and however experienced a driver Rolls may be, the
> success or failure of the enterprise must depend on the business
> management, and Rolls has no qualification for the conduct of a large
> manufacturing undertaking. The same remarks apply to me. These
> remarks do not apply to you, but unfortunately your name is not
> sufficiently known in London to instill confidence into possible
> investors. Very much the same remarks I think apply to Royce. Frankly
> I am of the opinion that our name as Directors are more or less
> worthless . . . what we want . . . is a board composed of men whose
> success is well known to the public.

Johnson had approached a Mr Singer with this possibility in mind, but
the latter was not interested and in his reply to Johnson enclosed a
cutting from a newspaper saying that Rolls was going in for 'aeronautics'. Johnson commented that 'from this I suppose he wishes us to infer
that he does not see the joke of investing money in a motor concern the
head of which is going to edit a paper devoted to "matters which are in
the air".'

Johnson concluded his letter with the suggestion that Claremont
should approach 'some of our best customers', amongst whom he
included A.H. Briggs and Walter Cliff, both of Leeds, and a Mr Tatton
Bower.[14] It seems more than probable that Claremont followed up this
suggestion, for it was Briggs, the wealthy woollen manufacturer and car
enthusiast, who came to the rescue when the issue was in danger of
failing. Johnson also mentions in this letter that he had discussed the
forthcoming issue with Lord Llangattock, Rolls's father, who had
thoroughly approved, from which he concluded that 'we need fear no
opposition in that quarter'; and it might be justly inferred that the
enterprise of C.S. Rolls Ltd was to some extent backed by Lord
Llangattock himself.

The results of the issue were awaited with what must have been
considerable anxiety in view of the unfavourable reception which it had
received in the press. The principal conditions of the issue were as
follows:

(1) No part of the subscription was to be paid in cash either to Royce
    Ltd or to C.S. Rolls, who were to be recompensed entirely in shares
    for both property and goodwill.

(2) A brokerage of 6d. per share was offered to the brokers and the bankers.

(3) A commission of 7½ per cent was offered to other people for the introduction of any prospective shareholder.

The Economist was attracted by the first condition, which was unusual, and drily remarked that 'it is a favourable point that the vendors take the whole of the purchase consideration in shares' and said no more. The *Financial Review of Reviews* was somewhat more critical:

> The objects are to further expand the business of Royce Ltd. of Manchester and of C. S. Rolls & Co. of London. These are both going concerns but their past earnings are not separately set forth. They should be. Estimates are merely given of what it is hoped the Company will earn under new conditions. The management are to receive under special contracts partly as salary and partly as commission, 15% of the net profits in excess of £10,000. The prospectus is not sufficiently explicit and future revenue is overburdened with the "rights" of management, as opposed to the interests of shareholders. A vague proposition which does not lend itself to comparison with any existing concern.

The *Motor Trader* sympathised with Rolls-Royce Ltd, which it hoped would prosper, but added

> We cannot help thinking the promoters have made a very weak appeal to the investing public. The price is steep for a name only a few years old, a computed £25,000 worth of machinery and plant, and an estimate of future prosperity about as tangible as the Aurora Borealis. . . . [The author was amazed] that an appeal so bereft of any form of inducement – outside personal confidence in the personalities which appear on the directorate – should have been made to the public at such an unpropitious season.

This was the market evaluation of what, from the investor's point of view alone, was to become one of the most successful concerns in the British motor industry.

The board had fixed a minimum subscription of 50,000 shares and had decided not to proceed with the issue if this number had not been taken up. On the last day the minimum figure had not been reached, and it seemed that the gloomy prognostications of the financial press were about to be fulfilled. De Looze however, had an idea that A.H. Briggs might be prepared to bridge the gap, and with Claremont's permission and encouragement he caught the next train to Briggs's home. The mission was successful. De Looze must have appealed successfully to the motoring enthusiast in Briggs's make-up and the prudent financier offered to put up £10,000 straight away. De Looze returned triumphantly with a cheque for this amount, and on 9 January 1907 Johnson was able to announce that £62,000 in all had been subscribed and that the company would proceed to allotment. Having solved the financial problem, Johnson and Royce turned their attention to the real work which lay ahead. The year 1907 was one of great activity in the motor industry and numerous firms had expanded their existing works or erected new factories. The largest vehicle plant in the country, not excluding the Argyll works, was opened at Coventry by Humber early in 1908. A considerable amount of new capital began to flow into the industry through private as well as public channels. From June 1906–June 1907 the total public issues raised £2.2 million out of a total authorised capital of £3.8 million. This amount was shared between 23 public companies and takes no account of capital raised privately. The investing public cannot have been unduly perturbed by the talk of French competition and the strong criticism of the omnibus failures.

In December Royce had produced an estimate of his output for the board for the following ten months of six or seven cars a month. In January he was asked to estimate the cost of the machinery necessary to produce 200 chassis a year, and £10,000 was provisionally authorised for machinery. The question of new buildings was being actively considered, and at the end of January Johnson and Royce were authorised by the board to select a site for the new works and to transact the necessary business which this involved.

In January 1907 Lord Herbert Scott, younger son of the Duke of Buccleuch, formerly a captain in the Scots Guards and a man who was well known in London society, became a director and the London sales manager. He was actively associated with the company until his death in 1944, eventually becoming chairman of the board in 1936. This appointment was obviously in pursuance of Johnson's policy of securing 'names' on the board, but this directorship was no sinecure. From the earliest years of the company's existence, the board followed a policy of drawing a large proportion of its directors from those who held important executive positions in the company. More of its directors graduated to the board through senior executive positions in the company than in any other way.

Rolls-Royce was thus launched on the basis of little more than the confidence, personality and ability of its founders, the willingness of a woollen manufacturer to take a risk, and a product whose reputation its makers were determined to establish and maintain.

The name De Dion Bouton was to France what the name Rolls-Royce was shortly to become to England. The one was the product of the enthusiasm of a French aristocrat, the Marquis de Dion, and the engineering ability of a French workman by the name of Bouton. Rolls and Royce were a strikingly similar combination. But Rolls-Royce possessed the significant additional advantage of Claude Johnson, a man of energy and ingenuity who brought to the company's future development the indispensable skills of that much underrated and maligned individual, the entrepreneur.

2 The Move to Derby

During 1906 the Rolls-Royce car was kept constantly before the public by Rolls and Johnson. The year started with a magnificent win in the Tourist Trophy race. Not content with victory on the TT course, Rolls followed this by driving the car up the steps of the building where the prizes were presented. Towards the end of the year he visited the U.S.A. and established both the reputation of the car and an agency in New York. On his return Rolls gave an interview to the press which resulted in a challenge from a distinguished American pioneer and manufacturer, E.R. Thomas (see p. 28), which he was unable to accept owing to a rather severe time limit. All this kept the car constantly in front of the public while Royce strove to improve it and to develop new ideas or improve old ones. This publicity was by no means exceptional. There were innumerable rallies and trials of every description, and success in these events was used by nearly all manufacturers as advertising material. The pace was fierce, but Johnson knew how to make the best of this situation and only entered the Rolls-Royce for the important events, or designed events of his own such as the 15,000 miles reliability run (the maximum distance permitted by the R.A.C. for such trials) which attracted even more publicity.

The strain of all this on Royce was very heavy indeed, but he did not complain. The 40/50 h.p. 'Silver Ghost', which was his greatest achievement, remained in production for a period of eighteen years in substantially the same basic form. It was designed in 1906, and must rank as one of the most outstanding motor vehicles of all time. The first sectionalised drawings of the engine appeared in print in December of that year. Royce himself shunned publicity as much as the others sought it for commercial reasons, but his name inevitably became known to the public. In February 1907 the *Manchester Guardian* remarked that 'in two years, from September 1904–1906 Mr. Royce obtained for his productions a foremost place in English industry, and a high reputation on the continent.' The *Manchester Guardian* omitted the equally important part played by Rolls and Johnson in securing that reputation.

The early success of the company, though dependent on the efforts of

6. The Silver Ghost, most famous of the breed

these three, was no less dependent on another factor of great importance. At the outset the company seemed to develop the ability to arouse the enthusiasm and loyalty of all its employees. Royce set the example and it was followed throughout the company. The names of Platford, Haldenby, Hives, Northey and Wormald were not widely known outside the company at this time. They were content to be members of a superb team, and it is the measure of a good team that its members demand no more than the achievement of the general objective and that they derive their real reward from the sense of co-operative endeavour. The human factor, the successful association of individuals, is the real foundation of any enterprise and this seems to have been intuitively appreciated and consistently recognised by the management of Rolls-Royce. One of the main problems facing the management in choosing a site for the new factory was the preservation of the team which Royce had built up, for however generous the capitalisation of the new company, this team spirit was something which it could not readily or rapidly re-create and its preservation was a central factor in the choice of a site. Though the issue had not raised all the capital that was expected it was decided to go ahead with the plan to build a new works designed specially for car production, as the Royce works could definitely not expand production further in the Manchester premises.

An estimate covering sites in four towns which he and Johnson had inspected was prepared for the board by Royce.[1] Several conclusions can be drawn from this set of figures. First, no consideration was given to the possibility of a further considerable expansion demanding skilled labour which was not already available or transferable. Second, the location of the principal suppliers of raw materials was not considered, the carriage referring presumably to the transfer cost of stocks already held in Manchester. Third, all four sites were in the Midlands. The London area, which was becoming increasingly popular in the motor industry and was the firm's principal market, was not seriously considered, if at all.

While these various sites were being examined Claremont suggested that the advice of a disinterested surveyor should be sought. It is possible that the Bradford site belonged to Briggs in view of his name being mentioned in the table, and that Claremont considered that the board might be prejudiced to the disadvantage of the company. He also suggested that the advice of an architect should be obtained over the building of the works, and that a consulting electrical engineer should advise on the contract for current and the installation of motors. The board rejected both the last suggestions but asked Mr Paul Ogden to report on the sites.

The surprising thing is that not one of the carefully considered sites was chosen. At the last minute a particularly attractive and pressing offer had been made by Derby, whose town council had heard that Rolls-Royce were moving from Manchester and set out immediately to persuade the firm to come to Derby. The Derby representatives were most persistent, and since their offer was attractive it was accepted and a large acreage of land purchased from the Osmaston Estates Company. Royce had always, where possible, followed the policy of training his own labour in Manchester, and little of this labour was lost in the move to Derby which took place by stages as soon as the new works were ready. He was not particularly concerned with the problem of securing additional skilled labour as he intended to expand the policy of training men in the works himself. The principal competitor for labour in Derby at this time was the Midland Railway works, but this had been established for some considerable time and it is more probable that the Midland Railway was afraid of losing men to Rolls-Royce than the reverse.

As soon as the land had been purchased Royce drew up an estimate of factory and building costs which came to £27,000, of which £15,000 was earmarked for machinery and £6500 for factory buildings. In June Royce reported that he had signed a contract for factory buildings for £9539, somewhat in excess of the original estimate. The total anticipated expenditure on buildings was expected to rise to £13,000 and the finance of this expansion presented a serious problem. The year 1907 was one of considerable financial stringency for the industry and the company. Some shareholders lost confidence and sold out when calls were made, and the failure of other companies did little to help matters. The commitments of the company were meanwhile constantly increasing, and the board was somewhat concerned with the liberal way Royce spent money on machinery which had always to be the best, irrespective of cost.

By the end of 1906 a sum of £4900 had been spent on machinery, and a further £7000 was spent in 1907. An unexpected liability was a serious underestimate of the bad debts of C. S. Rolls & Co., which were £1400 more than the transfer balance sheet figure. The Silver Ghost trial cost £519 more than was allowed, and by October 1907 commitments on capital account alone were estimated to be £22,000. This left a balance of capital available (including uncalled capital, but excluding stock and work in progress) of £31,700. The company had also embarked on a guarantee policy which was to prove a constant cause of controversy. The directors were all agreed that it was an excellent advertisement but were divided on whether or not it was worth the cost. This guarantee included a policy of modernisation and replacement, not only of defective parts, but also of parts which had been radically improved, either by Royce himself, or by other manufacturers. It was thus virtually in some respects a guarantee against obsolescence, inevitably costly.

Johnson's publicity policy was however as sound as it appeared, superficially, to be extravagant. The 2000 miles trial of the cars which were christened 'White Knave' and 'Silver Rogue' cost the firm some £3600, from which it was hoped that at least £2200 would be recovered from the sale of the cars. This and other similar trials not only secured for the car an amount of publicity far greater than would ever have been attained by the direct expenditure of a similar amount in the usual form of commercial advertising, but also provided Royce and his staff with the opportunity for long-range technical trials under excellent conditions.

7. The Silver Ghost chassis

But this type of publicity would not have been successful had it not been for the inherent technical excellence of the car. Its success was proportionate to the reputation which the technical quality of the car achieved, not only in public competitions, but in the hands of its numerous owners. Technical and commercial enterprise go hand in hand and this interlinkage is marked throughout the history of the company, which is clearly of a type whose success is closely dependent on the co-ordination of endeavour in both fields.

By January 1908, however, the financial position had deteriorated to such an extent that assistance had to be sought from the banks. Both this and a later occasion, when Rolls-Royce of America was formed, illustrate very clearly the great importance of adequate liquid financial resources in the formative stage of a company. Here was an organisation with a superb product, both technically and commercially. The design and development capacity of its staff was equally an assurance of continued achievement. Yet if the local branch manager of the London City & Midland Bank had not been prepared to take a chance and agree to an overdraft of £20,000 the move to Derby might have ended by the organisation stretching its resources too far and failing. It may well be argued that under this system there must be innumerable examples where similar combinations did not secure the assistance which they deserved, and failed. But though no statistical answer to this problem can ever be given, the case of Rolls-Royce, which is by no means exceptional, is a very weighty argument in favour of society maintaining the possibility of similar individuals taking similar risks under similar circumstances. Fundamentally it is an argument in favour of a system, not necessarily either capitalistic or socialistic, where the minority view can in some instances prevail. The actions consequent upon assuming the initiative are frequently those which would be condemned by a majority. The risks are frequently those which the majority consider too great. There can be little doubt that the destruction of the possibility of the minority view prevailing can involve society in a loss which may well be immeasurable. Even a partial destruction of this minority initiative can have grave consequences.

In 1907 Rolls and Johnson both took careful stock of the car market. Rolls went to America both to race and to explore the potentialities of the American market. His visit received wide publicity in the press, and on his return to England, his comments on the British and American motor-car industries aroused both interest and controversy. He considered that the prospects for British exports, despite the 45 per cent import duty then prevailing, were good. Exports of European cars to the U.S.A. had increased in 1907 by one third over the value of the previous year. Rolls was reported as saying that 'he considered that the Americans have not excelled the English manufacturers except in the case of small cars which they have standardised and can produce in large numbers thanks to automatic machinery. One reason why the American is so behind (in the more expensive range of cars), is the difficulty they experience in obtaining suitable steel at a reasonable price. The trusts will only accept orders for special steels in quantities of 1,000 tons.' He thought that the best American cars were made from parts from abroad, and concluded by advising British manufacturers to design their cars for the American market with a greater clearance 'to avoid the flywheel being bumped out' and that the track should be 4′ 8½″ so that they could 'travel on the tramlines and avoid cobbles'. Rolls told the press that his New York representatives wanted more Rolls-Royces than he could deliver, and that he had given a definite order for fifty cars to be shipped out in 1908. Most interesting of all however were his remarks on the unpopularity of British cars in the United States. There were three main reasons for this. The American owner was satisfied with his own vehicles and 'simply indifferent' to the quality of English cars; some very poor British cars had been shipped out, which had earned them a bad name; and the Selden Patent. Rolls was in favour of 'being with rather than against the combine in question'. The Association controlling this patent was 'an exceedingly close body . . . not very favourable to the admission of foreign firms'. (As Rolls-Royce was the only firm admitted within the previous fourteen months, this attitude is not surprising.)

This was the firm's first venture into the American market and in view of its great efforts during and after the First World War to capture in America the type of market which it had in part captured and in part created in England, the first impressions are interesting. The indifference of the American customer which Rolls observed was a factor which was very largely ignored in the later period.

The E. R. Thomas mentioned earlier had challenged Rolls to a 1000 miles reliability trial race from New York to Chicago, but though he made the terms of the challenge so difficult that Rolls was unable to accept, some of his comments on Rolls's analysis are prophetic.

> Mr. Rolls reiterates the same old cry used by English bicycle manufacturers in early bicycle days, that hand made English bicycles, though not having interchangeable parts, were superior to American bicycles. But American bicycles drove English bicycles to the wall in every country except tight little England, which is always loyal to its own. There is no reason to doubt but that history will repeat itself in automobiles.

In March 1908 some important decisions were taken by the board of Rolls-Royce. Claude Johnson had written an extensive report on the future of the English market which has unfortunately not survived. Its main conclusions were that there had been no falling off in the market for the six-cylinder car, that it was inadvisable to have two models, that a new model would cost thousands of pounds and that it was therefore a 'sounder policy to sell our present six cheaper than to make both the present model and a new four'. It was finally decided to standardise[2] the 'Silver Ghost', a difficult decision in view of the uncertain state of the industry and the multiplicity of models which Rolls-Royce, in company with most other manufacturers, had turned out. It is difficult for any manufacturer, whatever his product, to ignore the conventional pattern of market demand, and it is even more difficult to convince him that he himself is possibly creating that pattern. This decision encouraged a concentration of effort on the design and development of the Silver

Ghost which soon placed the car years ahead of its contemporaries and attained for it a reputation which did much to establish the name Rolls-Royce as a synonym for mechanical perfection.

8. The Silver Ghost 40/50 h.p. engine

The decision was taken in time to achieve great economies by tooling up the new Derby factory for the production of one model. The works were formally opened on 9 June, by Lord Montagu and the company settled down to a period of steady expansion. Its dividend performance had already surprised the sceptics who had looked with such disfavour upon the struggling company a few years previously, and its record in this respect was all the more startling by comparison with that of companies previously haloed with financial respectability.[3]

At a board meeting in July 1908, Johnson managed to persuade the directors that no further purpose was to be served by entering cars for public trials and competitions. He considered that these had served their purpose, that the company had established its reputation, and that the energies of management should now be devoted to maintaining it. The board agreed and since this decision has never entered its cars in any form of trial or competition. This policy has however been tempered by an understanding that it will provide technical advice and assistance where its products are entered in trials or competitions by individuals or organisations, if such assistance is considered to be in the interests of the company. At the time this was a rather bold decision, as another well known pioneer, S. F. Edge, had just asserted his belief that competitions were necessary for high-class cars to prove their worth and announced that Napiers would enter all the 1908 trials. Johnson foresaw that in these trials the standard car would soon be unable to compete without considerable modification and decided not to produce special cars for this purpose.

The last four years had been very strenuous, particularly for Royce, who fell seriously ill in September and was unable to attend several board meetings. From the earliest days Royce was a constant cause of anxiety to his colleagues. Eventually they realised that his ability was by far the firm's most valuable asset, and that its future would be seriously threatened by any permanent impairment of his health. In a very different way the last four years had their effect on Rolls by exhausting his interest in motoring, which had become almost established and prosaic. His interest turned towards aviation, a direction in which he could not persuade the board, or Royce, to follow him, and in July 1908 he asked the board's permission to become the consulting engineer of a company which proposed to manufacture airships. The permission was granted with the obvious resignation which accompanies a realisation of the inevitable.

Towards the end of 1908 trade conditions became seriously depressed. The board considered reducing the price of the car by £100 and, for the first time, discussed the question of producing a smaller car, either in addition to, or as an alternative to, the Silver Ghost. They decided instead to close the Lillie Hall premises in London and to centralise the staff at Derby. Despite the generally depressed conditions, however, a profit of £5389 emerged in 1907, which made possible a dividend of 6 per cent on the issued capital of £104,112. More surprising, especially to the City, was the declaration of a profit of £9063 in 1908, of which £5389 was employed to write off preliminary and removal expenses, and the remainder to maintain the 6 per cent dividend on the preferred shares. A conservative financial policy was thus pursued from the start. It was in fact a policy of the company first, shareholders second.

In February 1909, the subject of aircraft engines was mentioned at a board meeting for the first time. A suggestion was made, probably by Rolls, that 'this Company should acquire the right for the British Isles to manufacture the Wright Aeroplane'. It was turned down without further consideration. The aeroplane was still in the realm of fantasy, but the real reason for rejecting this proposal so unceremoniously was probably the shortage of working capital as well as the danger that Royce would overtax himself.[4] It appears, however, that Rolls, on his own initiative, had arranged for the company to manufacture the gearing for the War Office aeroplane and dirigible balloon without the formal consent of the board. Claremont protested strongly against this and moved a resolution 'that this Company not be allowed to depart from its standard work and manufactures without first obtaining the consent of the Board'. Thus the Rolls-Royce board had its feet firmly planted on the earth until the sudden impact of the First World War made it necessary, both in the company's own and in the national interest, for it to enter what at the time were regarded as exotic fields of engineering and manufacture. Prophecy is always dangerous, but the contributions which the company might have made to an earlier ending of the war had Rolls managed to interest his board in the aero-engine at this stage might have been exceptionally important. The lack of a developed and reliable aero-engine at the outbreak of war was a disaster of the first magnitude which nearly cost the Allies the war. It took almost three years to obtain quantity production of the first-class engine which Royce began to design when war broke out.

Claude Johnson, who was promoted from 'commercial' managing director to chief executive in March 1909, immediately embarked on a major reorganisation. At the general meeting in January 1910 it was announced that Royce had relinquished all executive duties in order to be able to devote his attention fully to technical matters. Throughout 1909 the board was seriously concerned about Royce. In May it was decided to appoint him to the post of engineer-in-chief, virtually created for him 'that he might devote all his time and energies to design, and to affording such technical assistance to the works as may be asked of him'. It is difficult, from reading this and a later, more emphatic, minute, to resist the conclusion that there was a twofold purpose in this endeavour to confine Royce's activities to design. His health had undoubtedly suffered from the strain of continual overwork, but in the factory he was somewhat autocratic and his disapproval, either of an employee or of his work, occasionally resulted in the man's instant dismissal. Though this

9. Portrait of Claude Johnson (*The Inverness Cape*) by Ambrose McEvoy

may now be regarded as an illuminating illustration of the eccentricity of genius, such action must have thrown a considerable burden on the works administration at the time.

Royce himself was a glaring example of 'too much experimentalism'. He was a poor production engineer, and production did not flow in a shop where he was working. Where there was any possibility of design improvement, production was immediately sacrificed. Output did not concern him and the logical solution was therefore to put this problem into the hands of those who were responsible for the firm's economic survival. Left entirely to himself, Royce would probably never have sold a car. He exhibited in his own special field all the intellectual qualities and failings of Lord Acton. Acton was never quite ready to write, Royce to finalise a design. The quality of the work which both of these men were able to achieve would probably have been seriously impaired had the necessity to produce been forced upon them. It was moreover well known that Royce regarded all administration as superfluous and the increasing size of what was generally, but to Royce accurately, termed the 'non-productive' staff at Derby was a source of constant irritation to him. He would have been content, it had been remarked, with a workshop in the middle of a field, and this, so far as it was possible, the management attempted to provide for him in due course by establishing his drawing offices in his own home at St Margaret's Bay, and supplying him with a team of draughtsmen. Thus was Mahomet kept at a safe and sensible distance from the ever-increasing mountain at Derby.

This relegation of design problems to virtually academic surroundings completely divorced from the factory was viewed with some misgivings at the time. But the results were found to be so successful that it became an established policy to maintain this physical separation of the design staff from the immediate surroundings and production problems of the factory. Royce was also encouraged to spend as much time as possible at his villa in Le Canadel on the south coast of France. This further development came about in an interesting way. The news of Rolls's death[5] in 1910 had a severe impact on Royce's already precarious health, which collapsed and forced him to undergo a major operation in 1911. Two years previously Johnson had bought a tract of land at Le Canadel and on this he had built a house named 'Villa Jaune' to which he now invited Royce to convalesce. Royce accepted and was so attracted by the area that he suggested building his own villa, an idea which found ready acceptance. There followed in rapid succession the construction of three further buildings, Royce's own 'Villa

Mimosa', a drawing office known as 'Le Bureau' and a small staff villa for resident or visiting designers known as 'Le Rossignol'. This early (if not the earliest) example of a deliberate separation of design and production staff was soon to be interrupted by the First World War, but the arrangement continued throughout one of Royce's most creative post-war design periods when he was to be responsible for both the Phantom chassis and the 'R' aero-engine.

By May 1909 the financial position had improved considerably. After authorising capital expenditure of £6263, a reserve of capital of £12,000 remained. Uncalled share capital amounted to £18,900. In September further capital expenditure of £10,780 was authorised, of which £9000 was for new plant. The available capital amounted to £14,312. In December orders were still greatly in excess of output, and a further £6000 was authorised in an endeavour to raise output to 25 chassis per month. Annual production was still well under 300 per annum. The financial position of the company seemed reasonably strong, and the board decided to apply for a quotation for Rolls-Royce shares on the London and Manchester Stock Exchanges. The profit for the year 1909 amounted to £19,993, allowing an 8 per cent dividend on the preferred shares and the modest amount of £718 for distribution amongst the ordinary shareholders, who had paid up £40,000. A reserve fund of £10,000 was created which, as Claremont explained at the annual general meeting, was due to the policy of the board, 'not to attract attention by the payment of large dividends, but to build up a solid business and effect a complete security of the capital invested in it'. In his speech, Claremont disclosed that the area of the factory was increasing steadily and added that the board were giving this problem their close attention because of their anxiety to avoid what he termed 'over-trading'.

> A works of excessive capacity [he said] is apt to induce excessive production, with the inevitable result of spoiling one's own market, since one in such a case is anxious to employ his works at their full capacity, which can only be done by so reducing prices and making goods in large quantity, which is often not to one's advantage.

These remarks were made despite the fact that deliveries were as much as six months behind orders, and Claremont justified them by saying that the Rolls-Royce was a product which could not be rushed. The board was in fact beginning to appreciate, if only in theory, the peculiar nature of their market. If price was reduced below a certain point, or production increased beyond a certain point, it was quite possible that demand would diminish and not increase. The product had become exclusive. The capital expenditure policy was formalised by Claude Johnson in a board minute in the following terms:

> As a general principle for the guidance of the General Managing Director in his recommendations for the expansion of the business, it is suggested that the capital expenditure in any year should not exceed half the balance of estimated profits during such period after deducting a sufficient sum for the distribution of dividends, the remaining half of such balance to be invested outside the Company in first class securities. In estimating profit as above mentioned account shall be taken only of orders received, although including those unexecuted. As far as can be arranged payments on capital expenditure shall not become due until the profits on the basis above described shall have been executed.

The policy was thus to invest up to half the profit in the expansion of the business, and it is clear from the above that the immediate availability of liquid cash resources was no longer the sole criterion, as it had previously been, of expenditure on capital account. The financial position now made possible the accumulation of general reserves to be invested outside the company until required, and to implement this policy Johnson and Lord Herbert Scott were appointed a financial sub-committee of the board.

On 24 June 1910 the Cooke Street, Manchester, premises were finally released, and the move to Derby may be said to have been completed. Royce regretted this move in later years. He thought that the board would have done better to move to the south, nearer the London market, in a more congenial climate and environment. Nevertheless, demand was strong, output increasing steadily and the pessimists confounded. Four years of peace lay ahead, though at the time anyone in the company, if not the country, would have probably said forty.

3 Consolidation and Expansion

In January 1910 Rolls surprised the board by asking them to relieve him of duties which he found 'irksome'. They accepted his resignation but very soon afterwards, on 2 June, he was killed in a flying accident at Bournemouth while attempting a spot landing in an aircraft which had not been designed to be flown at, or near, the stall. He had ceased to be a director of the company at his own request in April 1910, and his death was as great a loss to aviation as it was to the firm which bore his name, but during the last few years he seems to have had little influence on policy, which was now being directed almost entirely by Claude Johnson.

The company was now an established leader in its own field, and the name was already beginning to achieve an international reputation. Standard cars continued to compete with conspicuous success in various events all over the world, but the output was limited to 330 chassis in 1910. This was originally intended to be divided equally between the trade and the retail sales which the firm conducted itself, but Johnson considered it good policy to allot 255 to the trade even though this meant a reduction in the aggregate profit of £10,800, as a result of the sizeable trade discount, or £108 per car. Towards the end of 1910, Johnson again considered further expansion. At a board meeting he agreed that Britain was practically the only market and that 'circumstances might arise in the near future, such as financial depression, socialistic legislation, scare of war, etc.,' which might close this market. 'The Directors', he added, 'should be prepared to meet such a catastrophe as the closing of the Derby works through strikes, fire or war, by erecting a duplicate works complete with machines and tools in France, preferably near Paris.' The choice of France as an alternative centre of production is surprising and indicates that Johnson thought 'strikes and socialistic legislation' a more serious threat than war.

Claremont was opposed to any scheme which would involve an increased burden on either Royce or Johnson, as the erection of a new works would have caused. In his quaint and somewhat stilted language, he declared that he 'objected to spending on capital account one penny which could be avoided unless Mr. Royce agree to following his medical man's advice'. The problem of Royce had come to a head the previous September, when Claremont recorded a virtual ultimatum in the following board minute:

> In his [the Chairman's] opinion the disregard Mr. Royce showed for his health constituted such a serious menace to the stability of the Company that the Board was not justified in incurring any capital expenditure beyond what might be necessary for the protection of the business. That in other words Mr. Royce by his action was seriously hindering any enterprise or expansion of the business, and that . . . it was the duty of the Board, unless Mr. Royce would meet their wishes in this matter, to advise the shareholders of the situation since their subscriptions had been obtained largely on Mr. Royce's personality.

Royce – one imagines him a little astonished at this *tour de force* – agreed, on Johnson's suggestion, to accept his doctor's advice and to limit himself to design and development. The board's concern with his health appears to have been genuine, even though there was a definite desire to get him away from the shop floor, since quite clearly they considered the future of the firm to be dependent on his work.

In the event, expansion continued, although no attempt was to be made to manufacture cars abroad until after the war. Johnson thought primarily of France and India in his search for new markets, and not the United States, despite Rolls's predictions and enthusiasm for the latter country. The financial position early in 1911 allowed the payment of an interim dividend, and the board was sufficiently encouraged to launch a new company in France. This was to be known as Automobiles Rolls-Royce de France (henceforward ARRF) and the intention was to register it with an authorised capital of £250,000. The prospectus stated that the purpose of the new company was to erect and equip a new works in France where a chassis similar to that produced in England would be manufactured. These would be sold in France and Europe generally. Rolls-Royce of Derby would give all possible assistance to design and production, in return for which it was to receive £125,000 of which £80,000 would be in shares and the remainder in shares or cash. The parent company was to retain a majority on the board while it still held its vendor shares. It was estimated that the cost of equipping the new works would be £90,000 and that £30,000 would be required for working capital. The public was offered 170,000 shares for subscription, and it was decided not to proceed to allotment unless a minimum of 100,000 was subscribed. Only 2/6 per share was to be paid on allotment. The intention was to erect a works on the same scale as at Derby and it is remarkable that the further expansion of the Derby works to meet the increasing overseas demand was never considered.

The problem of security, was obviously uppermost in Johnson's mind. Economic considerations were completely absent.[1] They were not absent in the minds of the investing public, who regarded the venture as extremely risky, despite the record of the English company. The European market absorbed only a very small proportion of the Derby output and most people who gave any thought to the question probably did not regard France as being safer than England in the event of war. The issue was consequently a complete failure. Less than 20,000 shares were applied for, and the board decided not to proceed to allotment. Rolls-Royce itself had agreed to take up 100,000 shares.

A much less ambitious scheme was now put forward and adopted. It was decided to erect in France, under the nominal direction and ownership of ARRF, a repair works and chassis assembly plants for parts imported from England. Though the profits in 1910 were £37,700 and the reserve fund now stood at £27,500 the company was certainly not in a strong enough position to embark on a scheme which would have demanded a minimum of £50–70,000 of liquid resources, and might well have required a good deal more. What happened subsequently in the United States after the war might well have happened under far less favourable circumstances in France at a time when the development of the parent company itself would have been seriously affected. Branches were nevertheless established in France and India in 1911, and both consistently made a loss almost throughout their existence. This was later looked upon by the company as a justifiable expense to provide their customers in both countries with the high-class servicing available in England.

The guarantee to underwrite £100,000 of the proposed issue to finance French expansion was to bring about the first serious clash on the subject of financial policy. The company had no ready cash available to back this undertaking and the board contemplated raising the necessary money either by an issue of debentures or by a further issue of preference shares under its own name, ostensibly for the expansion of the English business. During 1911 some £17,500 was advanced to ARRF and, though the profit for this year was up to £50,000, the bank credit balance had become an overdraft of £30,000. Nevertheless the trading success of 1912, which yielded a profit of £69,000, plus the issue at a premium of £1 per share of the remaining unissued preference shares, enabled the company to convert the overdraft into a credit balance of £54,000. The two classes of shares had also been amalgamated into a single class of ordinary shares on the advice of a Mr Arthur Gibbs, a stockbroker in the City who was a friend of Claude Johnson and a substantial shareholder in Rolls-Royce. These shares all ranked, in effect, as a first charge on the company's assets, there being no mortgages, debentures or preference shares ahead of them. There were very few companies, if any, at this time, particularly in the motor industry, whose ordinary shares could boast such strength.

In April 1911 a concerted effort was made to obtain control of the company by acquisition of a majority holding by a group of financiers operating on behalf of Sir Maxwell Aitken (later Lord Beaverbrook) and two nominees (A.E. Bowen and I.H. Benn, M.P.). A block of 15,890 preference shares was acquired on 28 April, of which 7000 represented the holding of Royce Ltd, which had sold out, and a block of 20,000 ordinary shares, of which 15,500 represented the holding of Royce Ltd. The remainder were acquired from holders of small quantities of stock. By October 1911 the preference holding had been increased to 20,740. The group held the largest block of the issued stock, and was thus in a position to dictate its wishes to the board. This was apparently not realised by the board until the majority holding had been obtained. Aitken's group retained virtual control of the board throughout 1912[2] and appears to have acquired a further block of 10,000 shares of the new issue made in February of that year.[3] By 19 November 1913, however, the entire holding had been liquidated. It is significant that Sir Maxwell Aitken himself did not acquire shares until October 1913, after the events referred to below had taken place. This holding was small and not apparently connected with this manoeuvre in any way.

Sir Maxwell Aitken made it clear that he was opposed to any scheme of issuing debentures or preference shares to raise additional capital and that he was in favour of a policy of watering the capital of the company. He recommended Messrs Rowe and Pitman as an independent expert financial authority to advise on the best method, though he did not agree to follow their recommendations if he did not personally approve. This resulted in a reconstruction scheme along the following lines being suggested. The nominal capital was to be increased to £500,000 in 6 per cent preference preferred shares and £250,000 in ordinary shares, of which £250,000 preference and £150,000 ordinary would be issued. This was to be represented on the asset side of the balance sheet by a revaluation of goodwill which then stood at zero in the balance sheet. If the board assented to this scheme the majority shareholders were prepared to guarantee, at an underwriting charge of 4 per cent, a pro-rata issue of the 63,000 preferred ordinary shares which were still unissued at the date when these negotiations commenced. The majority group declared that they would support the proposals of Messrs Rowe and Pitman with their votes, but not necessarily financially, if the latter recommended a preference or debenture issue.

There was considerable discussion as to whether the board should commit itself to accepting such advice and the company's solicitors were strongly against such a precedent being established. Claremont himself was opposed to the whole scheme. Arthur Gibbs has made it clear that Sir Maxwell Aitken intended to transfer the registration of the company to Canada, since there was far greater scope under Canadian company law for the financial reconstruction which he apparently wished to carry out. On both these issues he was strongly opposed by Gibbs, who had promised Johnson that he would not give his assent to any scheme of this nature. Aitken was apparently not prepared to act independently and ultimately Gibbs was able to persuade him that the course he was proposing was most unwise, both from his own and from the company's point of view. The argument which finally convinced Aitken that this was so was that the registration of Rolls-Royce as a Canadian company would be most unpopular with the British public, who were already beginning to look upon the firm, if not as a national institution, then certainly as an institution which should not be transferred abroad without good reason. Since Aitken had already been subject to adverse criticism in the London press in connection with other enterprises and transactions he agreed to abandon the scheme and the syndicate ultimately disposed of its holding.

A finance committee consisting of the company's solicitors, an independent firm of accountants, a Mr Stockwell of Stockwell Williamson, the firm's own accountants, and the secretary, reported unanimously against the scheme and specifically condemned the proposal to inflate the goodwill. Sir Maxwell disapproved very strongly of the firm's solicitors being consulted on this issue and openly stated that he thought it wrong for the solicitor of the company to be the brother of the chairman of the board. The entire board disagreed and supported

Claremont strongly throughout the negotiations. After a series of protracted and tedious discussions, Sir Maxwell agreed to an issue of the balance of the preference shares at a premium of £1 per share, and later, much to his credit, withdrew unreservedly his statement about Claremont's brother. The company thereupon proceeded immediately with the issue which was underwritten by Messrs Rowe and Pitman for 2/6 per share. They were obliged to take up 32,960 shares, or just over half the issue. The total cost of the issue to the firm was over £6000, just under 5 per cent of the amount raised. Shortly afterwards, Mr G. Rowe and Mr Edward Goulding, MP.[4] were appointed to the board as Sir Maxwell Aitken's nominees.

The defeat of this takeover bid enabled the board to turn its attention once again to the more immediate problems of the organisation. The overdraft, which had reached £40,000, was paid off and a committee was appointed to investigate an allegation made by Sir Maxwell that the company was run on extravagant lines. He had been offered a seat by the board in October 1911 but the offer was refused. Nevertheless in December 1912 he changed his mind and intimated that he would now accept a directorship. Mr Rowe offered to resign in his favour but the other directors opposed this move and voted against the change, a step which must have taken some courage as Sir Maxwell's group still held a controlling interest.

This unexpected intrusion into the company's affairs was not without its beneficial aspects. The company was run, in the eyes of a good number of businessmen who came into contact with it, on generous lines. One of them is alleged to have remarked that his own firm would be bankrupt within three months if it used the embossed parchment notepaper on which Rolls-Royce conducted its general correspondence. This is significant in that it indicates the general reaction of the financial and business world to the name 'Rolls-Royce' and this reputation is likely to have influenced Sir Maxwell Aitken and his associates.

In other respects, however, the firm did not squander its resources. No palatial administrative headquarters were built, and the Derby factory and offices were designed and developed with a strict regard to the requirements of production and administration. No Grecian statues or Gothic stucco adorned the strictly utilitarian frontage on Nightingale Road, and in consequence the chairman was not involved in the awkward explanations which had to be made by the liquidators of such companies as Argyll Motors, where the disappearance of some £750,000 could not readily be explained.

The board was nevertheless stung by these criticisms into setting up a committee on establishment charges to take a close look at the company's expenditure. In due course, this committee reported that 'it was of the opinion that the business was carried out on very generous lines but that they were by no means prepared to say that it was unnecessarily so . . . they quite realised that it was perhaps the generous treatment which had so rapidly developed the business and brought about the present prosperity.'

The expansion of output continued steadily as new shops were erected and labour trained to the firm's exacting standards, but up to the outbreak of war it never quite caught up with demand and it was the firm policy of the board not to catch up with demand at the expense of the quality of the car. In February 1913 an additional expenditure of £8000 on tools was authorised to increase output by 50 chassis per annum, intended entirely for export. The demand for the car increased steadily particularly in Europe, but here there was a self-imposed limitation in that the company would not supply customers through foreign agents in countries where it did not have its own representatives or authorised agents. In March, however, it was decided to increase output by 125 chassis per annum, intended to bring in an additional profit of £14,000, or £112 per chassis. More land was purchased at Derby, a policy which provided a farsighted insurance against future expansion having to be limited by lack of space. It was decided simultaneously to manufacture chassis parts in batches of 200 instead of 100, as had been the practice previously, a policy which would eventually reduce batch costs but which had the immediate result of absorbing a further £30,000 of working capital in the purchase of additional material. The total working capital required for this expansion scheme came to £60,000 or £480 per chassis. Some £25,000 of this expenditure was written off out of profits, as the overdraft, partially secured by a mortgage on the land just purchased, was hovering around £50,000 in October 1913, and it was thought prudent to reduce it if possible to £39,000 by 1 February 1914 and £10,000 by February 1915.

The year 1913, which produced a net profit of £91,000 for the company, an increase of £20,000 on 1912, was also a successful year for both the French and Indian branches. The capital of the former had been reduced and, except for some shares held by the French directors, was completely owned by the parent company. ARRF owed the parent company £31,300 on capital account, and its accumulated losses in 1913 amounted to £4400. In 1913 however the sale of 122 chassis cleared the accumulated loss and provided a net profit of £10,600. The increase in output at Derby was viewed by the board as being solely on behalf of the continental business, and this figure was looked upon as a return on the sum of £84,000 which had been invested in this expansion. It is doubtful whether a factory could have been built in France to manufacture 150 chassis per annum for this figure, as much of the overhead expenditure incurred at Derby would have had to be duplicated. It seems unlikely that continental demand would have justified the erection of a separate factory in France at this stage.

In 1912 and 1913 the board, departing from its 'no competitions' principle, entered four cars in the Austrian Alpine Trials. In these trials, especially the 1913 event, the cars gave an outstanding performance, and this undoubtedly influenced Johnson's policy in the direction already described. The choice of a fleet of cars for the Durbar celebrations in India also had a beneficial effect on the Indian market.

Johnson may have been somewhat deterred by the failure of the French scheme to mature as he had planned, for in February 1914 he suggested to the board that he should personally explore the possibilities of the American market. The board agreed, and he sailed immediately. His visit was successful but no unduly ambitious schemes were launched. He reported on his return that there were 81 Rolls-Royces in the United States at this time and from this it would appear that C. S. Rolls's early estimates of the number of cars the American market would absorb were somewhat optimistic. Brewsters, a well known firm of coachbuilders, had offered to take 50 chassis a year for two years at the substantial discount of 20 per cent, but Johnson finally decided on a dual arrangement whereby Brewsters and an agent by the name of Schuette were to share this quantity between them. Schuette was described by Johnson as a motor-salesman and the son of a 'well-known and reputedly rich lumber merchant' who would know a great many wealthy potential customers. Brewsters had offered a showroom solely for Rolls-Royce chassis and cars, and Johnson had arranged for a Mr James Royce, one of Henry Royce's numerous Canadian relatives, to represent the company's interests in North America. An agreement was reached with Schuette which gave him the option, if his services were satisfactory to Rolls-Royce, of becoming manager of the New York branch at a salary plus 50 per cent of the branch profits. If he failed to exercise this option he was to have a further option to dispose of two-thirds of the number of chassis or vehicles which the company sent to the United States. This was a generous arrangement which offered Schuette every inducement to sell the Rolls-Royce. The outbreak of war destroyed any chance of his doing so, and his agreement had to be cancelled at great expense to the new company after the war.

Mention was made in May 1914 of an application for a licence to manufacture in Canada, but the purpose of this application seems to have been little more than to safeguard the company's rights in that country. In the same month a sum of £1500 was set aside for an exhibition in 1915, which illustrates how far from the minds of many businessmen was any thought of war at this time.

4 Alarms and Excursions

Though it would be absurd to say that the outbreak of war in 1914 was completely unexpected, the extent to which expectation had led to action of any description is well illustrated by what happened at Derby during the first few days and weeks following the declaration of war. The board met immediately and authorised Johnson to 'reduce the works wages to about one fourth by discharging about half the hands and allowing the remainder to work only half time'. He was otherwise 'to effect such economies as he thought desirable' and at the same meeting it was decided that the company 'would not avail itself of the opportunity now possibly arising of making or assembling aero-engines for the British Government'. The possibility had obviously occurred previously but although Royce had been pressed to convert his car engines for aero work he consistently refused to do so on the grounds that they were unsuitable. The argument that other engines were even more unsuitable was not the type of argument which convinced Royce. Though Royce and Johnson had developed at Derby one of the most advanced engineering organisations in the country, the above statements bear eloquent testimony to the fact that the entire organisation was staggered by the outbreak of war and that the management had no idea whatever of the important contribution which a plant such as theirs was likely to make to the war effort, or of the consequent financial significance to the firm.

It should not be forgotten however that the last major conflict in which Britain had been involved was the South African war, in which motor transport had played no part, and that neither generals, strategists nor politicians expected the First World War to develop into a prolonged and devastating conflict. The military significance of the internal combustion engine as a means of propulsion on land, sea or in the air (especially the last sphere) had hardly dawned on the consciousness of those whose imaginations and foresight, are supposed to qualify them for the role of military or national leadership. Even in Europe a war of manoeuvre was expected. Manoeuvre, according to military textbooks – those masterpieces of professional conservatism – was something carried out by divisions of cavalry and infantry. Motor-cars were thought to be useful for transporting high-ranking officers far behind the lines, where it would not matter if they broke down, and aeroplanes and balloons were considered to be of use to an army only as observation posts and no more.

It is not surprising therefore that the board should have thought that the company had been ruined by the outbreak of war, that it would have to close down as soon as the last car had been supplied to the last customer, and that it proceeded to act in a manner which in 1939, and even more so today, appears quite incomprehensible. It is evidence of the absence before the First World War of any theory of industrial mobilisation, of total war in the sense that it is now understood. Until 1914 wars had been regarded as affairs which employed armies that already existed, armies which might be substantially augmented if the need arose. In the First World War both the theory and practice of a national war effort were developed. The armies in the field could only be maintained by the efforts of the whole nation. In this national war effort Rolls-Royce, in both world wars, was to occupy a most strategic and significant position. The realisation that modern war demanded an industrial mobilisation as complete as the techniques and resources of the time permitted was brought about finally by the scale of the onslaught in France and the development of static trench warfare on an extensive front requiring millions of men and masses of equipment, but it was only the imminence of military disaster which forced an almost reluctant administration to accept the interdependence and equal importance of industrial and military mobilisation. The prevalent doctrine was very much that the army should be mobilised and its requirements 'bought' in the normal way. The process of buying was at first confined to the orthodox methods employed to supply the peacetime forces, and for the remainder of 1914 and 1915 this was the atmosphere in which the company had to work. It was a situation which demanded that the management should take the initiative if the firm was to survive, and this initiative was shown from the beginning as soon as Johnson and the rest of the board had recovered from the initial shock and given the problem some thought.

For some considerable time, however, the general commercial uncertainty which prevailed induced the management to adopt a short-term policy. This attitude is not as unreasonable as it may appear at first sight. The firm was solely a manufacturer of a high-quality luxury automobile. The market for these would undoubtedly collapse since the military demand for this type of car was expected to be negligible. Rolls-Royce had no knowledge of munitions manufacture, and had deliberately declined an opportunity to enter the aero-engine field. When war broke out staff and employees were having their annual holiday, and Johnson had a notice inserted in the *Daily Mail* instructing all employees to return home immediately and 'to observe the most rigid economy'. He spoke to the sales staff at Conduit Street and told them that the firm was being run on money borrowed from the bank, justifiable enough in normal times, but a position which tied the management's hands. On 31 July the overdraft was in fact £58,208, including £20,000 borrowed specifically for the purpose of buying land. Investments totalled £16,700 and customers owed £6100. Trade debtors amounted on the other hand to £47,000 and the net balance of assets over liabilities was £10,300. After summing up the financial position Johnson made the following statement:

A week ago the Rolls-Royce business and its property were worth a very large sum of money: I cannot say whether when the bank opens again on Friday the bankers may not take the view that the Rolls-Royce business is worth nothing at all, and therefore they may refuse to let us draw another penny from the bank. Anyone with their eyes open can see that the sale of Rolls-Royce cars must be absolutely stopped.

He expressed alarm at the amount of money still being spent on 'amusement', and advised the most stringent economy. All employees who had no reserve of funds were advised to stop paying their rent and to conserve their cash resources for food. They were told that accommodation would be provided for them and their families at the works if their landlords evicted them. Johnson advised men with wives and children to enlist, since their wives would thereupon obtain an allowance. In discussing the possibility of war orders Johnson said that he had contacted 'the Flying Factory of the War Office' (Farnborough) and had ascertained 'that we might possibly tender for the assembling of 30 engines and the making of a further 20, for which designs and specifications will be provided for us. There is a possibility of further orders which may keep our factory extremely busy, but I am only talking here of a possibility.'

With characteristic foresight, Johnson had also contacted the officer in charge of transport for the expeditionary force and had told him that Rolls-Royce had probably 100 chassis which could be taken over by the government. During the following week a tender was put in to the War Office for 100 chassis at £800 each, a figure on which a profit of £100 per chassis was expected. He went on to speak of the future and especially of America. He doubted very much if this market would last long, as he thought that America had been 'very hard hit' by the outbreak of war. There would not in any case be a market for Rolls-Royce cars as there was bound to be a glut of American cars and prices would slump. 'Unless', he concluded, 'we definitely get some aero work and money from the bank or Government to carry it on, it will be, so far as I can see, quite useless to open the works.' As the actual cash in hand amounted to £2794, this decision was not quite as shortsighted as it sounds.

At the board meeting on 14 August Johnson reported that he would have dispensed with the services of about 1000 of the staff by Saturday noon. The remainder were working 26½ hours a week, reducing the total hours worked to a quarter of what they had been previously. The commercial staff had been reduced to half, and the salaries of the remainder reduced by 50 per cent. These measures were expected to save £15,100 a year, a relatively small sum, considering their drastic nature. De Looze, the secretary, had meanwhile interviewed the bank manager in Derby, who had not imposed draconian restrictions on the firm's credit and had suggested merely that the company should not use the overdraft for the purpose of manufacturing cars for stock.

The War Office had meanwhile been urging Royce to reconsider his decision on the subject of aero-engines, and the suggestion was made that he should make 50 Renault engines. Royce and Johnson had been to Farnborough to interview Mervyn O'Gorman who was in charge of this work, and Royce decided to tender for it. This tender was requested by 18 August and the board considered that a price of £380 per engine would be suitable. Johnson had also been scouring the country to obtain sub-contract war work of any description, and by the end of August the works was engaged on a wide variety of munitions including shell cases, ambulance wagons and other munitions. Eight or nine hundred men were still employed producing eight chassis per week, but reserve stocks of material were being used up to maintain this output. The bank, in making its generous offer to provide 'whatever money the firm required' had asked Johnson what he intended to do. He replied that the firm intended to produce two experimental aero-engines and an experimental lorry which were estimated to cost £4500 in all. The overdraft was rapidly approaching the £80,000 mark, but thanks to Johnson's unceasing efforts orders began to increase, and at this same board meeting it was decided to employ the works full-time 'in order to be able to fulfil Government contracts'.

Conflicting decisions and the even more confusing lack of policy on the part of the supply departments of the government made the task of the management difficult. Following a national appeal for recruits on 3 September, Claremont wrote to Johnson saying that he was opposed to retraining any employee under the age of 35, or 42 if an old soldier, and that he thought that an announcement to the effect that the firm would not put any obstacle in the way of any man joining up would have 'the desired effect'. As early as 11 September, however, Wormald, the works manager, advised Johnson that 'we do require all the men that we can get hold of for war material, but we are not able to give preference to any of the men that we recently suspended, because, all of them, with the exception of two or three, have found other jobs. We are having to get the best men possible which is proving rather difficult.' The experience of Rolls-Royce in the labour field was by no means exceptional and by July 1915 the engineering trade group as a whole had lost 19.5 per cent of its workers. A deferment policy was not developed until considerable damage had been done to the war potential of the country.

The Rolls-Royce chassis as such was to play a spectacular part in the war as a chassis for armoured cars since its high strength factor and excellent design made it suitable for armoured car bodies without any extensive modification. The exploits of these vehicles, and of the aircraft which were later powered by Rolls-Royce engines, have been described elsewhere and are beyond the province of this study. But it is the aero-engine which from now on was destined to play an increasingly important part in the history of the company, and considering the success which it has enjoyed in this, the most difficult branch of the engineering industry, the reluctance with which the new field was entered is remarkable if only as a tribute to the modesty of the management at that time. Rolls's earlier suggestions had been consistently turned down by the board because of their concern for Royce, especially when he refused to go abroad to Le Canadel after the war had broken out and insisted on staying in England and devoting himself unceasingly to the design of aero-engines. The possibility of making magnetos had also been considered and rejected in the first few months of the war, for on 8 October Claremont wrote to Johnson saying, 'I certainly think we could make a name for magnetos; but again I dread the strain on Fred.' The danger of Royce overworking and collapsing was the limiting factor at this time and everything possible was done to give him the maximum opportunity to work uninterruptedly on design in the most congenial surroundings possible. He was segregated as far as possible from all administrative and financial problems, often to his great annoyance. These problems were shouldered by Johnson to an ever-increasing degree.

The position of the firm in the present situation cannot be fully appreciated except in relation to the general state of confusion which prevailed in the aircraft and aero-engine industries, the word industry being little more than a courtesy description at this time. The hub of the structure was the Royal Aircraft Factory at Farnborough, established in 1905 as an experimental unit capable of designing and constructing its own aircraft and engines. There were in addition twelve private aircraft firms, with a total output of about 100 aircraft per annum. Three of these specialised in seaplanes. In addition, two leading ordnance firms held contracts for aircraft designed at Farnborough. Nearly all the British-designed engines (designed either by Farnborough or by enthusiastic amateurs) were in the experimental stage, and the reliance on French engines was complete. Not one British aircraft engine was actually in production or anywhere near it. Farnborough had not been given authority to design its own engine until 1913, when a sum of £5000 was allowed for this purpose, and the position was so desperate in the early part of 1914 that a joint military and naval competition was held to encourage new designs. This was won by the Green engine, which was ultimately a complete failure. Farnborough had also designed an 8-cylinder 90 h.p. engine to replace the 75 h.p. Renault (the RAF 1) which was put into production early in 1915 with five firms including Daimlers, a 110 h.p. radial (the RAF 2) and a 200 h.p. water-cooled engine (the RAF 3). The second was dropped when war broke out, and the third was handed over to Rolls-Royce and Napiers for development and completion. Sunbeams had developed two engines of 100 and 200 h.p., both of which were unsuitable because of weight and petrol consumption, and the most powerful engines, as yet only in the design stage, were a 12-cylinder air-cooled V engine (the RAF 4), which Napiers were to produce in large quantities before it had been proved, and a 12-cylinder version of the RAF 1. Not one of these engines was in production until 1915, and in the first months of the war the dependence on French engines was total.

The magnitude of the problem was further increased by the German monopoly in the design and manufacture of magnetos, but stocks of these lasted until July 1916, and complete engines were far scarcer than magnetos in the first months of the war. By 1917, however, both magnetos and ball-bearings had become the main factors limiting engine output, which was then at the most critical stage.

The deplorable state of the air arm was partly the result of official prejudice but equally the result of the relative infancy of aviation as a whole. Pre-war development of aircraft for military purposes had been presided over by a body known as the Joint Air Committee under the chairmanship of Col. J.E.B. Seely, Secretary of State for War, but neither this body nor any of its successors, until a relatively late stage in the war, had executive powers commensurate with its responsibilities and only the major strategic revolution brought about by the use of air power on the Western Front (brought home to everyone by the bombing of London in 1917) was sufficient to overcome the opposition of the War Office and the Admiralty to the creation of an independent air arm under a separate Ministry equivalent in authority to either, and responsible for the design, development and supply of aircraft to all three services.

August 1914 various aircraft firms had been allotted to each service by verbal agreement, there remained little possibility of constructive co-operation between the services on the problem of aircraft supply. Rolls-Royce was handed over to the Admiralty under this arrangement after negotiations between the DGMA (War Office) and DAD (Admiralty).

The problem of shells and munitions, which was considered to be far more immediate and urgent, occupied the attention of the existing supply organisation to the exclusion of all else for several months. Orders for aircraft engines were spasmodic and uncoordinated and usually controlled by relatively junior officers. It is to the very great credit of the Admiralty, however, that it foresaw the need for high-powered engines (mainly through having to operate seaplanes) and appointed production officers with exceptional discretionary powers to those firms which had Admiralty contracts. The Admiralty, alone in the initial stages, was responsible for encouraging the production of Rolls-Royce, Clerget and Sunbeam engines as well as for an expansion of engine production facilities in France which saved the situation on the Western Front in 1917. The official policy on supply before the outbreak of war had been 'so far as possible to keep a constant minimum number of hands employed at the Royal Factories allowing a margin for sudden expansion in an emergency, and to throw the fluctuations on the trade'.[1] In the first three years of the war, the inadequacies of this policy were soon revealed.

Rolls-Royce was also approached on the subject of shell manufacture directly by the War Office and asked to tender on 6 September. A tender was immediately put in but it was not accepted. An early offer to make machine guns was also refused by the War Office.[2] The policy at this stage was to concentrate orders on large and well-known munitions firms such as Vickers, Firth, and Beardmore, and efforts were made to divert labour from the smaller concerns to the large munitions works. Many valuable months were lost before these policies were changed.

The position of the firm at the end of 1914 and early in 1915 is somewhat confused, and the few remaining documents relating to this period do little to clear the picture. On 23 September 1914 the Admiralty ordered 20 chassis and 20 Renault engines, and the total value of war orders on the books stood at £20,000. There was, however, a heavy demand for chassis from all quarters, and it was decided to continue building six chassis a week to meet this demand. By 31 October 1914 a sum of £57,700 had been spent on machinery 'in anticipation of government contracts' and it seems that the management had recovered from the initial shock of the war and had begun to reorient themselves and the firm towards the new situation. Salaries were restored to normal and a scheme of allowances to dependants was inaugurated. The British Expeditionary Force had requisitioned all Rolls-Royces in France, and in October the company established a special repair base in France. Royce had turned down, on technical grounds, the RAF engine which he had been asked to produce, and negotiations with the Admiralty started in December 1914, Admiralty policy being 'to buy aircraft, engines and spares in any available market'.[3]

The Royal Naval Air Service was not directly represented on the Board of Admiralty, but an Air Department had been established under Commodore Suetter which was responsible for advising the First Sea Lord, and Commander Briggs, a most energetic and enterprising member of this Department, had the initiative to encourage Rolls-Royce from the outset.[4]

On 3 January 1915, an order for twenty-five 200 h.p. Rolls-Royce engines was received from the Admiralty, the price being fixed at £950 per engine. This engine was the Eagle, and a further 75 were ordered by the Admiralty on 19 April. The price on this order had been raised to £1151 per engine, and the total value of the orders now amounted to £109,690. The Admiralty intimated that it considered this price to be 'special' and that a reduction was expected on new orders. The immediate concern was output. The third and final Admiralty order in 1915 was for 300 Eagles and 100 Hawks (a smaller 75 h.p. engine). The horsepower of the Eagle had been raised to 250, and the price to £1300. The total sum involved in these orders was £453,000.

On 26 November 1914, Claremont wrote to Johnson saying that he thought the volume of orders was 'quite bewildering'. Apart from the Renault engine, one hundred of which were manufactured, these orders were for chassis and general munitions. But from the outset Johnson seems to have appreciated the potentialities of the aero-engine industry, and the possibility of Rolls-Royce securing a lead in this field. 'Do you really think it is wise', he wrote to Claremont on 4 January, 'to mention the fact that we are making aero-engines? It may act as a suggestion to other motor manufacturers, and would therefore increase the number of our competitors in the aero engine market.' This somewhat narrow view of the position of Rolls-Royce versus the rest of the industry was by no means inconsistent with the general attitude of industrialists at this time, who frequently found it difficult to resolve the contradictions of national and business interests. But Johnson always considered his business interests in the broader context of the national interest. In his appreciation of the role of air power, and of the best methods of organising the national production effort towards this end, he established a Rolls-Royce tradition which was to endure.

The conflict between the Admiralty and the War Office early in 1915 is reflected in the confusion existing in the Derby works. Claude Johnson's brother, Basil, who later succeeded him as managing director for a brief period, had recently joined the firm and had made many visits to the various air departments of the Ministries in an attempt to remove some of the anomalies and contradictions of policy and programme. He seems to have had no success, for on 15 March Claude Johnson wrote to the War Office mentioning negotiations over a scheme whereby Rolls-Royce was to manufacture 100 RAF six-cylinder engines and the receipt of the Admiralty order already referred to for Eagles.

If we were to make the RAF engines at the date previously contemplated it would mean that the manufacture of that engine would follow immediately after the manufacture of 25 Rolls-Royce engines of 200 h.p. and therefore all the tools, machinery, etc., engaged in the manufacture of the Rolls-Royce engine would have to be dismounted in order to be replaced by the tools necessary for the manufacture of the RAF engine. This dismounting of tools and mounting of new tools would, of course, mean a serious loss to the nation, as compared with the far more efficient programme of our continuing to manufacture the 200 h.p. Rolls-Royce engine for the Admiralty, and we therefore suggest that in this time of the Empire's great need you may be able to arrange to have the 100 RAF engines of 100 h.p. manufactured in some other firm which is already engaged in the manufacture of these engines, or by some firm which is not at present engaged in the manufacture of engines for the country.

These arguments were lost on the War Office, which seems to have been somewhat affronted by the letter. In a subsequent letter to Lt.-Col. W. S. Brancker, Johnson tried to correct this impression. Rolls-Royce had been invited, he said, to tender in August, but the tender had been declined. It was then suddenly accepted by telephone on 29 January and an amended order was received on 23 February. Certain requirements in the specification needed modification and work did not start until 13 March. The Admiralty had meanwhile ordered Eagles and Rolls-Royce suggested that they might persuade the War Office to cancel their order. The War Office refused to do this and both types were manufactured, resulting in a smaller output and additional expense.

Johnson was quick to appreciate the fact that important policy decisions affecting the management of Rolls-Royce were now being made elsewhere. Provided that the war departments purchased the whole of the firm's output they were clearly in a position to dictate what should be produced. These decisions were determined by strategic considerations, which were not the concern of the Rolls-Royce management, and by broad considerations of economic policy which, at this stage of the war, were within the theoretical province, but as yet beyond the effective control of Parliament and the Cabinet. In a letter to Claremont on 31 March Johnson revealed the approach of Rolls-Royce's senior management towards the problems created by the war.

> The British military authorities in France and England wish to impress upon the public that the date at which the war will be finished is regulated mainly by the supply of the Munitions of war.
>
> The earlier the war is over, so much the better for Rolls-Royce Ltd., for instance our French Company alone is costing us £1,000 a month.
>
> The Admiralty assures us that the delivery by our Company of 200 h.p. Rolls-Royce aero-engines is of the greatest importance in connection with the general scheme for the finishing of the war, and in

addition to the 25 of these engines already ordered, are anxious for us to make a further 75, and in addition a considerable number of new 150 h.p. Rolls-Royce engines. The War Office are anxious for us to make at once 100 of the RAF factory aero-engines, and if we had the equipment would be glad to give us an order for 8 of these engines per week for the whole of 1916.

In the face of this national situation there are two alternative courses which we can take. Firstly we may say that in order to maintain the Rolls-Royce business of motor cars we must insist on making a number of motor cars for pleasure purposes and therefore will only devote a proportion of our works to satisfy the urgent national demand for war engines; or secondly, we may place the whole of our equipment entirely at the disposal of the nation.

I do not think it is possible for any firm of repute to take the first course. Furthermore, I do not believe that it would be to the interests of the shareholders to take the first course. And, if we take it, the Government would force us to do what in my opinion we should do graciously. At present we are adopting the second course. By the end of July our business as motor manufacturers will be suspended except for the manufacture of two chassis per week, which will, it is believed, be required by the Government. Our works will otherwise be devoted to the manufacture of perhaps twelve aero-engines per week.

Johnson now accepted that the direction of the company was virtually in the hands of the War Office and suggested that the shareholders should be informed of the consequential change in the powers and status of the board.

As regards the price of the goods which we manufacture for the taxpayers I do not believe that it is our duty to use our wits to take out of the taxpayer's pocket the highest possible price for the supply of goods which are devised to bring this war to an end. It may be said that other companies are engaged in this endeavour. Personally, I should be very ashamed to stand up before the shareholders and ask them to commend the General Managing Director because he had succeeded in extracting from the pockets of the already over-burdened taxpayer a price for war goods which has enabled me to put large profits in the pockets of the shareholders. We are, therefore, quoting prices for war goods which are intended solely to cover the cost of labour and material, to cover our established charges at home, but not abroad, and to provide a moderate profit.

A copy of this letter was sent to Arthur Gibbs, still a substantial shareholder in the company and a long-standing personal friend of Johnson, for his comment and criticism. The last paragraph provoked a controversy between Claremont and Johnson which is not without interest, particularly to those who take the view that the entrepreneur in such a situation is so dominated by the immediate requirements of profitability that no other considerations are ever allowed to affect the decisions which really matter. Johnson thought that the chairman should make an announcement warning the shareholders that profits might fall because the firm was engaged on war production. He suggested that it should take the form:

> *Patriotism Before Profits.*
> *Important Announcement.*
> Temporary suspension of the production of Rolls-Royce cars.
>
> At the request of the War Department Rolls-Royce have designed special engines for war purposes. The Government orders for these and other war engines are so extensive that Rolls-Royce Ltd., have arranged temporarily to suspend the manufacture of the well known Rolls-Royce chassis excepting those for Government use. Messrs. Rolls-Royce are, however, booking orders on their waiting list. Such orders will be dealt with in strict rotation as soon as Government requirements have been fulfilled.

This was not to Claremont's liking. He suggested that the phrase 'patriotism before profits' should be left out and a new sentence included which stated that war work had absorbed practically the entire output of the firm and that the aero-engine had achieved a considerable reputation. Johnson disagreed since both the suggested additions were misstatements. 'War work', he said, 'has not practically absorbed our entire output since the outbreak of war and . . . our aeroplane engine has no reputation because no one except ourselves had tried it.'

In his reply, Claremont again took exception to the phrase 'Patriotism before Profits'. 'Although we personally may have such views', he wrote, 'I think it would be inadvisable to allow the shareholders the opportunity of saying we had adopted them at their expense.' Johnson discussed the matter further with Arthur Gibbs, who had replied in the first instance that he was in agreement with Johnson that the shareholders should be informed.

10. Ernest Claremont

I agree with you [said Johnson] that I think it is most important we should not allow shareholders to run away with the idea that because we have secured government contracts they must look forward to good profits. I would much sooner that they should understand now that we are putting patriotism first and profits second. I am not afraid of what the shareholders will say, seeing that if only the shareholders are to lose by the policy, we, the administrative directors, will also lose very heavily. No shareholder has the right to demand that we should make exorbitant profits when our only customer is the British taxpayer. Furthermore, as we have placed the factory entirely at the disposal of the Government, we are no longer in a position to dictate as to how the factory may be used to produce the greatest amount of money. It is now left to the decision of the Government officials as to the military importance of the articles they wish us to make, and the numbers in which they should be made, and the order in which they should be made, and Government officials study military importance rather than factory efficiency.

Arthur Gibbs agreed with the principle that if any announcement were made it should be the whole truth, but two members of the board, Rowe and Goulding, opposed any announcement before the balance sheet was published. In a long letter, Rowe elaborated his views to Claremont:

As regards the course Mr. Johnson proposed to take, I can see no sort of benefit in it to anybody except to the market speculator. If Mr. Johnson's object is to prevent people buying the shares, he is automatically hurting those shareholders who may wish to sell. If he has no thought of the market value of the shares, then there is no object whatever in his advertising extremely harmful matter to the share-holders . . . We have no earthly right to tell the shareholders that we propose to adopt a purely patriotic attitude and manufacture stuff for the nation at a loss. Our duty is simply to try and make our orders for national departments work out with a reasonable profit.

The confusion which the term 'reasonable profit' arouses is still a serious hindrance to accurate analysis. It implies the assessment of a given result – the accounting profit determined in accordance with a given set of rules and conventions – within a certain ethical framework. The idea of what is 'fair' in a given situation must vary with innumerable economic, political and sociological factors. It will vary as between different economic systems and will be profoundly influenced by the historical circumstances which have provided the environment in which the economic system has developed.

An accounting profit is itself dependent on the suitability and accuracy of the methods employed to measure changes in the real assets and in the economic life expectation of a firm or industry, and the choice of these methods, and their application, for example in laying down rates of depreciation and in valuing stock, frequently involves the exercise of judgement within fairly wide limits.

Substantially different results can be obtained by employing different methods of accounting assessment in the same situation, and perhaps more important, by different individuals employing the same methods of assessment. Thus an accounting profit or loss results from an attempt to measure with reasonable accuracy, for practical and comparative purposes, the achievement or failure of an enterprise in the economic environment within which it has to operate. The term 'fair profit' is thus as meaningless in the United States as it is in the Soviet Union. A measure dependent on judgement cannot be fair or unfair. It can only be accurate or inaccurate by the best known standards. Profits can be exceptional, average or below average. It is an index of efficiency in the employment of economic resources. In wartime, under a private-enterprise system such as that which operated in the First World War, it can either be sufficient or insufficient in the absence of other controls to induce the entrepreneur to undertake the production assigned to him. The strength of the inducement necessary will vary under such a system in time of war no less than in time of peace. There is no such thing as an absolute standard of reasonableness. But, if more resources are used in the pursuit of any economic objective than are created, whatever the economic system the wealth of society will steadily diminish.

Although the imprecise term 'a reasonable profit' is often used as a final arbiter, Rowe had very direct and uncomplicated views on this issue. 'Mr. Johnson', he continued, 'seems to think that the market price of the shares is a matter of only secondary importance, but it surely is the only thing which the shareholders think about.' While Rowe may well have underestimated the patriotism of a good many of the shareholders, his emphasis on the need to maintain the investor's confidence was a factor which no board of directors, even in wartime, could altogether ignore.

Had Johnson devoted too much effort to an attempt to resolve this difference of opinion, it would have involved him in all the controversy and complexities which those responsible for determining the rate of profit in Ministry of Munitions contracts uncovered when they attempted to establish general principles. Neither the Treasury Select Committee on National Expenditure nor the Colwyn Committee were able to formulate a satisfactory definition or to lay down any general principles for the guidance of Ministry officials responsible for settling the terms of contracts.

The controversy over profit and the appropriate attitude towards it in wartime reveals the top management of the company adopting the posture of trustees, not only towards the interests of shareholders, but towards employees and society as a whole. Thus, while Johnson undoubtedly intended that Rolls-Royce should survive, he appreciated that it was not in the long-run interest of the firm itself or of the system of private enterprise that it should do so or even appear to do so at the expense of the nation. His final letter to Claremont makes his position quite clear:

> Mr. Rowe seems to regard the price of shares as being of primary importance. On the other hand, I regard the price as being of secondary importance as compared with a determination of the Board to hide nothing from those who have placed money in the Company . . . Leaving the national welfare out of the question, we should consider the new policy a good policy to adopt because we are contributing to the effort to secure that the war shall cease at the earliest possible date, and to arrive at this goal must be for the greatest benefit of the shareholders and bankers.

On 19 May 1915, the board decided to send out the notice, but at its previous meeting the directors had approved a resolution proposed by Johnson himself that £10,000 should be expended on the purchase of raw material in readiness for the resumption of car manufacture. There is no suggestion that this action was thought to be in the least inconsistent with a strong determination to further the war effort to the utmost. It was reported on 10 March that production was 80 chassis behind schedule, mainly through shortages of material. Every effort was made to obtain the material, as the delay was estimated to be costing £150 a week. A resolution which was to have far-reaching results was passed by the board to the effect that

> As it was probable that the supply of certain raw materials for work other than government work might at any moment be cut off in this

country, Mr. Nadin be sent to America to purchase what the Company could not obtain here.

Johnson also reported to the board that he considered that the works 'were not being run at their highest efficiency so far as war work was concerned,' and said that he proposed to see the departments about it. Civilian chassis were still being produced, the great majority for sale in the United States. By the end of October 1914 33 chassis had been sold there for £29,300, on which a gross profit of £6200 had been realised. It was reported early in 1915 that the only market for Rolls-Royce cars in America was in the East and that Americans in the West seemed to be 'content with inferior goods'. Johnson continued to press the sale of cars in America right up to the entry of that country into the war, and when production at Derby finally ceased he purchased second-hand cars in England to be reconditioned and shipped to America.

The evidence available suggests that 1914 and 1915 were years of comparatively unintensive production. This confusion, lack of policy and failure to employ effective capacity in the best possible way which was characteristic of the company in the first eighteen months of the war reflect the even more serious failure of the entire national supply organisation towards the end of 1914 in the field of shells. This became progressively worse in the early months of 1915. The air war, however, had not developed as rapidly or proved as decisive as the war at sea or on land, and it was not until the middle of 1916 that the serious military consequences of the ineffective development and deployment of British air power became clear to those responsible for policy and, in due course, the public.

The first intimation that the government appreciated the necessity for full industrial mobilisation came with the passage in March 1915 of the Defence of the Realm Act, a measure which had been enacted because engineering plant, and above all, skilled labour, could not be diverted from private to government work without compulsory powers. The negotiations with the unions had brought no improvement in the situation as the latter were opposed to dilution, geographical and technical mobility, and the surrender of restrictive practices when they thought that these measures would only enhance the profits of employers. Mere promises by government officials that the *status quo* would be restored at the end of the war gave them no reassurance. Negotiations, particularly between the Engineering Employers Federation and the Amalgamated Society of Engineers and government representatives created a fog of mutual suspicion, emotional prejudice, mistrust and lack of confidence which even the emergency of war was unable to dissipate.

In February the Prime Minister, then Mr Asquith, appointed a Committee on Production which presented four reports. The first three dealt largely with restrictive practices in industry which the committee considered would have to go as soon as possible, and the fourth contemplated the possibility of the state taking full control of certain vital industries, such as shipbuilding, for the duration. The committee came to the conclusion that profits would have to be limited by legislation and government control of armament firms extended, solely in order to secure the concessions demanded from the trade unions.

Winston Churchill, then First Lord of the Admiralty, was the first to suggest a far-reaching plan of state control to avoid, as he put it, 'further meddling with the labyrinthine difficulties concerning different classes of labour'. In a memorandum to the War Cabinet, he proposed that the government should take over the whole of the mercantile marine and shipbuilding industries, and that a subsistence allowance of £1 a week, with a guarantee of three to six months' employment, should be paid to men moving to a new district.

This proposal was too far-fetched, even for a British government at war and, by the middle of 1915, its place had been taken by the familiar stalking-horse, a plan to limit profits. When the coalition government was formed in May, Mr McKenna began to prepare a bill for an excess profits tax. Meanwhile the declaration of its intention enabled the government to reach agreement with the trade unions in March and to persuade their leaders to suspend demarcation rules and other restrictive practices. But the results were disappointing and no effective control of either employers or labour became possible until after the passage of the Munitions of War Act in July.

Within the limitations of the existing system, miracles of improvisation were achieved, but they were not enough. The Munitions of War Act prohibited stoppages or lockouts, made arbitration compulsory and provided for 'controlled establishments' in which profits would be limited and in which wages and salaries could not be changed without official sanction. Restriction of output rules were suspended. The board of directors of a controlled establishment became in theory, and frequently in practice, the agent of the Ministry of Munitions, and were obliged to run their plant in a prescribed manner.

When Rolls-Royce was made a controlled establishment on 12 August 1915, Claremont immediately instructed Johnson and De Looze to take stock so that a balance sheet could if necessary be drawn up at this date. Wormald, the works manager, advised very strongly against this step, as the annual stocktaking was not due until October, and an additional stocktaking would not only have disorganised production but might have caused unrest amongst employees who had been asked to put forth their maximum effort. They might easily have questioned the necessity for a procedure which they always associated with the ascertaining of profits. The proposal was consequently shelved. The domination of British national and industrial policy, even in this time of national crisis, by this deep-seated misunderstanding of the function of profits thus revealed itself at an early stage in the history of the company.

Apart from general measures such as these, the development of the supply organisation in the Ministry of Munitions, and in the Admiralty and War Office supply departments which preceded it, did not affect the aircraft or engine firms until January 1917, when the responsibility for aircraft production was transferred to the Ministry. Sir William Weir had proposed this in a memorandum to Lloyd George as early as May 1916 but no action was taken at that time. In 1915, the various aircraft and engine firms proceeded quite independently and negotiated directly with the individual air departments of the War Office and Admiralty, between whom there was no effective liaison before the establishment in February 1916 by Mr Asquith of the Joint War Air Committee under the chairmanship of Lord Derby. This committee was set up to resolve conflicting ideas of policy between the two services, but as it had no real executive powers, and its authority was ill-defined, it succeeded merely in becoming a focal point for the clash of opinion, and on 3 August 1917 Lord Derby resigned.

The absence of a coherent national supply policy is again clearly reflected in the operations of the company during the latter part of 1915 and early 1916. The Eagle had run its first test in December 1914 and the Falcon and Hawk were designed in 1915, a tribute to the tremendous energy which Royce put into this work from the outbreak of war until the end of 1915. But it was not until June 1916 that the first squadron of F.E.2d's was equipped with Rolls-Royce engines, the first deliveries of Eagles having begun in October 1915. The production of chassis, different types of aero-engine and sundry munitions continued throughout this period, and though the firm was sufficiently occupied to cause Johnson no financial concern, he was fully able to appreciate both the cause and the cure of the relative deterioration of Allied air power on the Western Front. By 4 August 1915, the output of aero-engines for the

11. The Falcon engine

Admiralty reached 30 a week, though this figure is difficult to reconcile with official reports of deliveries. But there was still surplus capacity at Derby and in August Johnson travelled to Copenhagen to negotiate for the rights to manufacture the Madsen automatic rifle. On 28 August an order for 5000 of these was received at the price of £100 per gun.[5] The terms of the contract[6] which was drawn up illustrate the type of compensation which companies considered necessary to justify their entry into certain fields of munitions manufacture. All additional capital expenditure was regarded as a direct cost of production which must be recovered by including it in the total price of the contract. Thus any plant and buildings erected for the purpose of fulfilling such contracts were looked upon more as a liability than an asset. A similar principle was applied by Rolls-Royce to the first Admiralty contracts, and became a subject of considerable controversy with the finance and contracts branches of the Ministry of Munitions at a later stage.

Towards the latter part of 1915, Johnson began independent negotiations with sub-contractors. As will be seen later, he had very definite ideas on how aero-engine production capacity should be increased which he proposed to put into practice on his own accord. Several prospective agreements were considered by the board on 5 October. Brazil-Straker, a firm which had manufactured the Straker-Squire car before the war, had been asked to manufacture the Hawk and other aero-engines. The Standard Motor Company of Coventry had been asked to manufacture the Falcon and Eagle. Sheffield-Simplex, another pre-war manufacturer, was asked to consider taking over all Rolls-Royce's munition work. At the next board meeting, on 26 October,

12. The F2A Bristol fighter, powered by the Rolls-Royce Falcon

Johnson stated his intention of concentrating all aero-engine manufacture and assembly at Derby, a farsighted step in view of the fact that existing orders failed to utilise fully the resources of the Derby factory. Negotiations were also opened with Messrs Allen & Co. of Bedford and with Armstrong-Whitworth. The development of a wide-ranging sub-contract system by a private organisation was very much contrary to prevailing official ideas of how such things should be done, and negotiations over several of the more important contracts, such as that with Standards, broke down when the War Office informed Johnson that direct orders were contemplated. The negotiations with Brazil-Straker are however of interest, as this firm did eventually manufacture for the company.[7] The Admiralty order to Rolls-Royce at this time was for 775 engines at a total contract price of £865,500.[8]

The proportion of this order which Johnson wished to sub-contract to Brazil-Straker was 100 Falcons and 95 Hawks, at the same prices, involving a total sum of £169,200, on which it was agreed to advance Brazil-Straker 12½ per cent or £21,152. An agreement was concluded under which Brazil-Straker was to produce six engines per week, and to make no other engines while they produced Rolls-Royce engines. Rolls-Royce was to receive half the profit, Brazil-Straker having an option on future production up to the capacity of their works. Rolls-Royce was to supply the material and certain completed parts and to pay Brazil-Straker their production wages plus 150 per cent for establishment charges. The balance between this total and the price paid to Brazil-Straker by the government was to be divided equally. The government agreed to advance Rolls-Royce 12½ per cent on the total order, and of this it was agreed that Rolls-Royce would advance £10,000 to Brazil-Straker.

This contract, which is typical of those entered into at this time, involved the main contractors, Rolls-Royce, in the same difficulties which the government itself encountered in practically all cost-plus contracts. Throughout 1916, Brazil-Straker made continual calls on Rolls-Royce for cash to finance its operations and at a board meeting on 2 June a loan of £22,500 was discussed. Johnson commented on that, 'that the working of the existing contracts with Messrs. Brazil-Straker caused so much discussion and dissatisfaction and absorbed so large an amount of energy that he had come to the conclusion that it would be more economical for the Company to sacrifice all possibilities of making profits by the employment of Messrs. Brazil-Straker as sub-contractors,[9] than that the present arrangements should continue.' He suggested that after completing 20 Falcons Brazil-Straker should produce Hawk and Falcon parts on the following terms:

(1) Brazil-Straker would order all material;
(2) The government would pay Rolls-Royce, who would pay the sub-contractor;
(3) Rolls-Royce was to have inspection rights;
(4) Brazil-Straker was to receive 'all the monies paid by the Admiralty to Rolls-Royce in connection with the work done by Brazil-Straker

from the beginning of the arrangement between the two firms, except monies owing by Brazil-Straker to Rolls-Royce for material supplied or work done and a sum of £32 per Hawk and £64 per Falcon'.

On 10 March 1917, a letter was received from Brazil-Straker explaining the reasons for their request for a further advance of working capital. These were that there had been no profit on the Hawk owing to lack of output; that there had been unforeseen capital expenditure of £10,000 on Rolls-Royce work which Brazil-Straker 'not being main contractors were unable to provide for in later tenders'; that Brazil-Straker had repaid the capital sum advanced (£10,000) while working with no profit; and that a large stock of lorry material unsuitable for engine manufacture had been left on Brazil-Straker's hands when they accepted the Rolls-Royce work.

Rolls-Royce were not satisfied with this explanation, particularly in view of a disturbing report from one of their inspectors which stated that Brazil-Straker 'were going to considerable trouble to ascertain the actual profile of the cams used on the camshaft, measuring and recording all possible features in connection with the Hawk and the Falcon, producing a special car engine identical with the Hawk, and modifying a Curtis engine with Rolls-Royce features'. It is not surprising that firms such as Rolls-Royce were reluctant to encourage others to manufacture their products and preferred to see several firms making parts rather than one making a complete engine, particularly when the former policy was more likely to achieve a greater output. At a conference held on this problem at the Ministry of Munitions between Johnson, Commander Briggs and others, Johnson refused to provide further financial assistance to Brazil-Straker, and on 31 March, the Ministry advised him that all further orders would be by direct contract as soon as the second hundred Hawks and the two hundred Falcons then being put through were finished.

Rolls-Royce claimed to have lost heavily through this contract, and in their reply placed the blame fairly and squarely on the authorities who had insisted on them going straight from design to manufacture. An allowance of £35 per engine on an order for 250 Eagles and 200 Falcons about to be placed was requested in order to extinguish the loss. This method was quite frequently applied by contractors who had incurred substantial and unexpected losses. Since an *ex gratia* payment on account of past miscalculations was obviously impracticable, the loss was incorporated, sometimes quite openly, in the price of the new contracts. These negotiations illustrate the difficulties which arose between manufacturers who were actual or potential competitors in the same industry and were suddenly called upon in time of war to pool their knowledge and resources. Neither the Ministries nor Rolls-Royce had acquired much experience in the control of sub-contractors and in the successful co-ordination, both physically and financially, of an extended series of operations. Johnson was dismayed by the failure of the Air Board to understand the principles underlying a proper sub-contracting programme, and in June 1917 an invitation from the Air Board to present his views on the problems of increasing engine production gave him his opportunity. A memorandum was prepared in consultation with Royce and copies were sent to all members of the Air Board.

The memorandum began with a survey of the machine gun controversy. Soon after war broke out Johnson had suggested to the War Office that the war would be fought with machine guns and that Rolls-Royce, although it had no experience of these, or any other weapons, was prepared to throw its resources into this urgent field of production. The War Office replied that 'Only one firm, Vickers, makes these (i.e. Maxims) and I am told here that their output, which is of course, very large, is amply sufficient for all Army and Navy requirements.'

Eight months later, said Johnson, the War Office was begging him to undertake the manufacture of machine guns (presumably the Madsen rifle). He then took up the thorny question of the repair of aero-engines. This had become a serious problem since all these engines had to be repaired at Derby, ostensibly because parts were not interchangeable.[10] This situation was bound to interfere with the production of new engines. Rolls-Royce had pointed this danger out many months previously and had asked the War Office for permission to build and equip a special repair shop to handle this work. This was refused, mainly on the ground that a completely equipped shop was available at Armstrong-Whitworths. In his evidence to the Bailhache Committee[11] on this subject General Henderson stated

> Messrs. Armstrong had a shop, tools and labour; therefore I wanted to employ them. We failed. I would have infinitely preferred to do that rather than extend Rolls-Royce.

In a memorandum on this subject prepared for the Committee on

Imperial Defence it has been stated that the main reason for the breakdown of these negotiations was Armstrongs' unwillingness to accept a condition laid down by Rolls-Royce that they should produce only Rolls-Royce engines during the remainder of the war.[12]

Johnson thought that the failure to equip this shop, which would have increased output by 500 engines a year, was inexcusable.

Not only do we believe that the nation will require the 500 extra engines which this shop could produce, but we believe that they will so far require war engines that it is probable that there will be no Rolls-Royce automobiles built for 20 years or more after the war because of the necessity of building and keeping up-to-date an air fleet of a magnitude which it is difficult to conceive at present.

Johnson then turned his critical attention to the wider problems of production. He first proclaimed his faith in competition.

The weakness of most Government departments is that they are not subject to competition such as that which exists between firms who have to produce articles of merit in order to exist. A business which had no competition gradually becomes slacker and sleepier.

... The keener the competition in producing the most efficient articles the better it is for any business ... The fact that there are two distinct departments responsible for the Navy Air Service and the Army Air Service respectively, has created the most stimulating and healthy competition.

Johnson was no doubt favourably disposed towards this otherwise impracticable arrangement since the development of Rolls-Royce engines had been so very largely due to Admiralty encouragement and orders at a time when the War Office did not appear to be interested or to know what it was doing. He was most critical of the principle of submitting engine designs to other designers for criticism and selection. This he thought was as unfair to the designers themselves 'as it would be to ask a mother to judge a baby show in which her child was competing'.[13] The next paragraph attacked the rumour that manufacturers were opposed to Farnborough because it gave the government a check on prices. 'We have never heard', he said, 'of such an objection nor thought of such an objection, nor do we believe that the trade has ever had in its mind such an objection. The story is the invention of politicians.'

Administration of the sub-contracting programme was the next target. He advised the Air Board to extend the works of existing manufacturers rather than build new factories. Existing works could expand their output considerably without having to duplicate indirect labour and organisation to the extent that would be required if new factories were established. Men, machine tools and material were the three factors limiting output. Skilled men should, he thought, be brought back from France, and machine tools 'removed from the scene of their idleness to aero-engine shops'.

Standardisation was the cure for low engine output, and Johnson was justifiably critical of the practice of giving production orders for untried engines. The full import of this criticism was not appreciated until 1917 when one engine after another which had been put into production proved a failure. 'So far as the present war is concerned', he said, 'it would be perhaps unwise to rely on newly invented engines and wiser to choose the best existing engines and concentrate on manufacturing them in the largest possible numbers,' a lesson which had to be learnt again in 1940. After classifying the existing engines, he suggested that there should be six main factories, one to each engine, and that all the rest should act as sub-contractors. The central factories would order all material and distribute it to their sub-contractors who would concentrate on part production thereby becoming proficient as well as reducing the demand for skilled labour. The next recommendation was particularly drastic, coming from a businessman, but strictly logical considering the existing situation which Johnson had described. Rolls-Royce, he said, held the view 'that in order to make proper use of the engine manufacturing capacity of this country, it would be necessary that the government should have power to direct any factory as to what work it is to perform and that it should use the power'.

His next target was the inflexibility of the existing contract system. Sub-contractors were unable to operate as cheaply as the main contractors, and it was absurd to expect the main contractors to bear this loss.

In a business such as the supply of urgent war material in which the saving of TIME rather than the saving of money is essential, the Air Board may properly be required to state roughly what its financial requirements are, and should be empowered to spend money within these limits. Existing contracts departments under the Treasury are controlled by men who have been reared in red tape and by systems which make rapid achievement impossible. They have been surrounded by regulations until many of them have become as timid as chickens and as obstinate as mules. Any man with a sense of duty who has served under the Treasury would be failing in his duty if he did not acquire these qualities. It is imperative in the interests of victory that the war operations of the Air Board should be free from interference by Treasury officials.

This was an understandable reaction to the familiar 'red tape' phenomenon of war but hardly a practical proposal. It was to recur in 1940 when Lord Beaverbrook, for a brief period, jumped over the traces and blew most of the fuses in Whitehall.

There was nevertheless considerable room for improvement within the existing systems. Johnson condemned the system of paying contractors fixed prices, since contractors would fix prices to cover themselves against all contingencies and no real national economies would be achieved in consequence. He suggested that contractors engaged on purely government work should be paid their peacetime profits plus certain expenses, and added that Rolls-Royce had a detailed scheme if the Air Board wished to examine it. This has unfortunately not survived.

Johnson's memorandum concluded with a discussion of morale. The life of the average workman producing parts was drab and monotonous and he rarely if ever saw the final product. He suggested that the disinterest and discontent that was bound to develop under such a system could be eliminated or at least reduced by the following steps:

(1) Naming every 20th (or some such number) engine fitted after the works which made it. Where aircraft had participated in important battles their names should where possible be mentioned in the news bulletins.
(2) The Air Board should supply films and lectures to tour the production centres.
(3) Those employees who attained a certain standard of performance should be presented with badges declaring 'that they have worked well voluntarily towards winning the war'.

It was not until the disasters of 1917 had brought about the most drastic reconsideration of this problem that some of the excellent ideas in Johnson's memorandum, particularly on sub-contracting, were put into practice. The acceleration of technological advance in wartime creates economic and administrative problems that are not always appreciated at the time. A failure to relate this advance to production can result in a misdirection of resources such as occurred when several hopelessly underpowered engines were put into large-scale production. They were obsolete by the time quantity production had started. The problem which faces any manufacturer of a product which depends on advanced technology in peacetime is greatly magnified in time of war, but the cost of misjudgement in the latter case may well be at best a prolongation of the war and at worst defeat. For the firm itself, there is no escape from the economic risk associated with these technical judgements, even when much of the cost is underwritten by the state, so long as its main resources continue to be employed. But the conflict between the 'planners' and the entrepreneurs is often accentuated under these conditions by the fact that men such as Johnson often owe their achievement to their capacity to assess risk and form critical judgements in circumstances which they frequently understand much better than the officials temporarily charged with this responsibility.

5 The Years of the Eagle

At an Admiralty conference on aero-engines in September 1915 it was agreed that Rolls-Royce should spend £99,000 on new buildings and machinery to enable orders for an estimated total of 775 engines to be met. A sum of £25 per engine was allowed as additional compensation for this capital expenditure. Orders actually confirmed in 1915 had amounted to a total of some 500 engines, of which three hundred Eagles and one hundred Hawks had not been ordered until November.[1] The contract for a new aero shop costing £16,900 was signed in December and machinery to the value of £14,600 was ordered. Negotiations were meanwhile being continued with Armstrong Whitworth and the French government. The terms for both contracts were identical, namely a minimum order of 1000 engines, and a royalty of 10 per cent on the invoice price. In January 1916 the negotiations with Armstrong-Whitworth ceased, as Johnson was not satisfied with the way in which the scheme was proceeding. This, as has been seen, caused some criticism. A conference was arranged, at which Claude Johnson, Bonar Law and Sir David Henderson were present, in an attempt to persuade Johnson to change his mind, but he persuaded the others that the company's attitude was justified and no further steps were taken.

Preparations were meanwhile being made to start production of the Madsen rifle, and in January the board confirmed expenditure amounting to £104,000 on tools for both Madsen and aero production. The overdraft by this time had reached the record figure of £194,000. This was soon exceeded, and the borrowing powers conferred on the board in the articles of association had to be increased by special resolution at the annual general meeting. No sooner had the shops begun to tool up for the Madsen rifle production than the powers that be changed their minds. In March 1916 Johnson learnt that the cancellation of the contract was under consideration at the War Office, and in April the final cancellation was received. The War Office had been strongly prejudiced against the gun by a fatal accident which occurred during its demonstration to a group of senior officers, but the main object of the cancellation was that the firm should devote all its resources to engine manufacture.

On 9 April 1916, the Admiralty ordered a further 200 Eagles, and in June a further order for 300 Eagles, 300 Falcons and 100 Hawks was received, the total value of the last contract being £1,092,000, the largest order the company had ever received. The total number of engines ordered by the services in 1916 was 1600, valued at £2,431,700. The prices fixed under these contracts were the source of considerable controversy at a later stage. The capital expenditure involved in the orders placed in the first six months of 1916 amounted to £120,000, to be covered by a payment of £25 per engine. The total capital expenditure directly on war production which had been incurred, or was about to be incurred, at this time, was £247,000, a large proportion of which had been provided by the bank overdraft. In July, the Admiralty intimated the possibility of an order for 1800 more engines, and it is interesting to note that the board contemplated the recovery of the whole of this sum, £90,000 having already been recovered on existing orders. A calculation was made that if £25 per engine was to be allowed, additional orders for 4100 would be required to compensate the company for this expenditure, which was considered to be of no future value whatever to the firm.

The increasing superiority of enemy air power on the Western Front had created a strong demand in the press for an inquiry into the question of air policy and supply, and the government was forced to set up the Bailhache Committee to inquire into the administration and command of the air services. This committee issued two reports in August and November, and while they more than vindicated the strategic employment of the R.A.F. in the field and bestowed high praise for the work which had been done with limited and obsolete equipment, the supply organisation and the general application of national resources to the production of air power came in for very strong criticism.

In May 1916, the decision was taken to establish an Air Board, and Lord Curzon, a member of the Cabinet, became its first chairman. The representative of the Admiralty had to be a member of the Board of Admiralty, and the army representative on the Army Council. Despite the rank of its members and the importance of its task the Board was not granted any significant executive powers. Its terms of reference were nevertheless considerably wider than those of its predecessors, and the energy and influence of Lord Curzon enabled the Board to do good work. When it was established each service still supplied itself with aircraft through its own supply department, and the control and direction of aircraft production was not in the hands of the Ministry of Munitions

13. The Eagle aero-engine

except in so far as the Ministry's general controls over material and manpower applied equally to aircraft firms. More direct limitations (as distinct from positive direction) applied to firms such as Rolls-Royce which had been made controlled establishments. Positive controls were developed and extended by the Ministry of Munitions for other munitions and supplies where extreme shortage had virtually obliterated competition between the services, making a central co-ordination of production and supply imperative and demanding an allocation between the services which was determined by the broadest strategic considerations.

In August 1916 Lord Curzon became aware that the Admiralty had sought and received Treasury sanction for an expenditure of £3 million on aircraft and engines without having obtained the Air Board's approval. The Rolls-Royce orders undoubtedly formed a substantial proportion of this total. Lord Curzon immediately protested in the strongest terms to the War Cabinet. The Admiralty in reply stated that their Lordships considered that the matter was not one which came within the province of the Air Board, and Mr Balfour, then first Sea Lord, wrote an indignant rejoinder in which he maintained that the Admiralty was responsible for the Royal Naval Air Service. In conclusion he pointed out that the Admiralty had been created 'some generations before the Air Board' and that its framers 'had not the wit to foresee that it would some day be required to carry out its orders in subordination to another department'.

14. The De Havilland DH9A, powered by the Rolls-Royce Eagle Mark 8

It is surprising that Mr Balfour expected them to have foreseen the evolution of air power, but the fact that they did not possess this foresight was not an argument against the creation of an independent Air Ministry responsible for the new military power which was weighing so heavily in the scales on the Western Front. But though both of the established departments did so much to delay and impede the formation of an independent Air Ministry it was entirely due to the farsighted judgement of the Admiralty, acting independently and in its own interests, that Rolls-Royce engines were developed at a time when they were relatively unknown, and under conditions which were later considered to be unduly favourable financially to the firm. The Admiralty built a factory in France to supply 8000 Hispano-Suiza[2] engines for the British and French governments, having rightly judged that the engines produced by the British aircraft industry under the existing organisation would prove inadequate either in quantity or quality. The really serious supply failure late in 1917 was due, however, to errors of technical judgement rather than to a failure to anticipate demand.

Towards the end of 1916 German air superiority became a really serious threat on the Western Front and Sir Douglas Haig made an urgent appeal for a further 20 squadrons, specifically requesting a hundred Rolls-Royce engines and fifty Hispano-Suiza for the purpose of equipping two D.H.4, two Bristol Fighter, and two Spad squadrons (Eagle, Falcon and Hispano). The Admiralty, which up till then had had the lion's share of Rolls-Royce output, released fifty-five of its own engines and four squadrons which were placed at Sir Douglas Haig's disposal.

At a cabinet meeting on 16 December, shortly after Lloyd George became Prime Minister, it was decided that the powers of the Air Board would have to be widened, that the Admiralty should be represented on it by the Fifth Sea Lord, and that the Ministry of Munitions should also be represented. Of greater immediate significance was the decision to transfer the responsibility for the design and supply of aircraft to the Ministry of Munitions itself. At the end of December 1916 the Air Board became a Department of State, and a new division of function between the Air Board and the Ministry was laid down. The Ministry became responsible for production and inspection during manufacture and the Air Board alone was made responsible for design, production totals and allocation of aircraft. The Board itself was strengthened by the appointment of Lord Cowdray as chairman, and Sir William Weir and Mr Percy Martin (managing director of Daimlers) as members, but its authority was still disproportionate to the functions which it was expected to perform.

This belated and inadequate reorganisation of the home front could do nothing to stem the tide of disaster flowing in the early months of 1917. There was great disquiet in the country and public opinion demanded more drastic changes. The establishment of the Royal Flying Corps was increased during the last six months of 1916 from one to two hundred squadrons, and it was estimated that a production of 2000 engines per month would be required. Production at the end of 1916 reached a figure of 600 engines a month, though since many of these engines were underpowered and obsolete the mere numerical increase over 1915, in which only 5363 engines all told were produced in England (1864 in addition were imported from abroad), is not much indication of any effective increase in strength. Although the engines on order had been increased to a total of 19,000 at the beginning of March 1917, nothing that could now be done in England could have any substantial effect in France until 1918. Lord Curzon when President of the Air Board had opposed the placing of large orders for aero-engines. In November 1916 he had expressed the view that 'the increasing exhaustion of the belligerents rendered it doubtful whether a supply in the latter half of 1917 or early 1918 would be of any service for the purpose of war . . . We were every month coming nearer to the point of general exhaustion beyond which the war could not go on.'[3]

The Ministry of Munitions' task was to develop production for the interim period of 1917, to organise the increase in production required to recover air superiority in France and to build up a strategic bombing force capable of seriously damaging the German industrial system. The first step was to establish a Department of Aeronautical Supplies based on a nucleus of staff from the corresponding sections in the War Office and Admiralty. This department of the Ministry became very largely a self-contained unit housed in the Hotel Cecil in London and took several important decisions almost immediately. The first was that the number of engine types should be reduced from 51 to ten, and the second was to allocate the highest priority to aircraft and aero-engine construction. Both these decisions were recommended by Johnson in his memorandum in June 1916. The factors limiting output at this stage of the war were alloy and carbon steel, ball-bearings (for both of which Great Britain was dependent, much to the distress of the Foreign Office, on Scandinavia), silver spruce and skilled labour. The supply of aircraft, however, was greatly in excess of the supply of engines, and the 1917 reorganisation did little to alter this situation.

When the decision to give top priority to the expansion of air power was made, the number of engines was reduced to eight. Of these, four – the Sunbeam 6, the Sunbeam 8 (Arab), the Hispano-Suiza and the B.H.P. – were in the 200 h.p. water-cooled class. Two were rotaries, the 130 h.p. Clerget and the Bentley, and two, the Rolls-Royce Eagle and the RAF 4A were in the higher power class. In the first group the largest orders were placed for the Sunbeam Arab, of which 4400 were ordered from the Austin, Napier, Sunbeam and Lanchester companies. Two thousand B.H.P.s were ordered from the Siddeley Deasy company and large orders were placed for the RAF 4A and the Hispano-Suiza. In all 19,700 engines were ordered but, with the exception of the Eagle and the Hispano-Suiza, most of these engines were either technical or production failures.

Early in 1917 Rolls-Royce received a further Admiralty order for 250 Eagles (17 March) and authority to order materials for 150 Eagles and 75 Falcons (12 May). On 29 June the first direct order for 500 Eagles was received from the Ministry of Munitions, which increased it to 650 on 7 July. Nineteen hundred Eagles in all were ordered in 1917 and a further 100 in January 1918. Of this total of 2000 engines it was intended that 1500 should be manufactured in the United States.

The magnitude of the orders placed for Sunbeam, Hispano, B.H.P., RAF 4A, Clerget, Le Rhône, Bentley Rotary and Rolls-Royce engines induced a degree of optimism in official quarters which was such that an actual surplus of aircraft was expected in 1918. In the event the Rolls-Royce programme in England and the Hispano programme inaugurated earlier by the Admiralty in France were the only two which came anywhere near expectation, and had these failed as disastrously as all the others, including the Liberty programme in the United States, the expansion of Allied air power in 1918 would have been impossible, and the war in all probability prolonged for another year at least.

Early in 1917, however, the management of Rolls-Royce came into direct conflict with the Air Board. In October 1916 Johnson had reported to his own board that the expansion of aero-engine output was being hampered by 'other work', which was in fact repair work which the management considered should be carried out only at Derby. Foreseeing the inevitable expansion of repair work consequent upon the ever-increasing number of Rolls-Royce engines in operational service, he sought the authority of the Air Board to erect a special repair shop at an estimated cost of £125,000. This suggestion had first been made in his memorandum in June, and the request was repeated in August without success. In February 1917 Rolls-Royce output was falling seriously behind schedule, and on 9 February General Branckers reported to the Air Board that a number of D.H.4 Squadrons were unable to proceed to France for lack of engines. On 12 February Sir William Weir reported to the Air Board that of the 42 Falcons and 32 Hawks promised in January only 26 in all had been delivered. General Henderson thought this was because Rolls-Royce had concerned themselves with increasing the power rather than the output of their engines, but Mr Percy Martin thought that the firm had done well considering the facilities at its disposal. At the earlier meeting Lord Cowdray had amended his intention of putting in his own manager in the works, but had the sense to realise that this would not work. Mr Martin visited Derby and on 4 April reported to the Air Board that the output was 25 engines a week and that he considered an output of 30–40 engines possible. No decision was reached on the repair shop, and in June 1917 Sir William Weir again raised this thorny problem at the Air Board but without success. On 14 July however the decision was reversed and the board was instructed to proceed.

15. Eagles in production

The Air Board was also considering the possibility of increasing Rolls-Royce output by standardising one engine, the choice lying between the Eagle and the Falcon. The Director of Air Supplies suggested that the engine chosen should be the Eagle and that the Falcon should be replaced by the B.H.P., Hispano and Sunbeam. Royce did not agree with this proposal,[4] and though the Air Board agreed that Rolls-Royce should concentrate on the Eagle, which was to be converted to an output of 360 h.p. after the next batch of 150 engines had been completed, this was not done. By October, the shortage of Eagles had become so acute that an instruction was issued that no modifications whatever were to be introduced.

A considerable stumbling block in the negotiations on the question of a repair shop had been the nebulous question of capital expenditure, and a telegram sent to the Board by Claremont throws some light on this problem.

> You will recollect we some months ago refused to proceed with the repair shop unless the Government accepted our claims with regard to excess profits; they now threaten that unless we accept terms less favourable amounting in several years to £30,000 they will erect a repair shop themselves. I consider this would be disastrous, and owing to extreme urgency I ask your immediate authority by telegram to make the concessions and obtain the best terms we can.

This controversy on the subject of recoverable capital expenditure was by no means confined to Rolls-Royce. The exceptional rate of capital expansion in the aircraft industry, the extent of state intervention caused by the fact of the Ministry being the sole customer, and the incidence of forms of taxation whose full effects were appreciated neither by the state nor by the managements (whose policies were determined by the range of the economic spectrum which was visible to them) were factors which created a most confusing situation.

In discussion with the Admiralty in the latter part of 1916 Rolls-Royce had put forward a series of proposals:

(1) That all construction and plant for the government should be depreciated by 35 per cent per annum (a figure based on the estimated difference between pre-war and existing prices);
(2) That the £25 per engine allowed on contract should be considered as further depreciation;
(3) That an additional depreciation of 20 per cent on plant and 5 per cent on buildings should be allowed on the original cost less the 35 per cent already deducted under (1).

A table of figures at this period shows clearly[5] the light in which the management regarded this problem. Claremont and De Looze, who represented Rolls-Royce at the conference in August at which these claims were put forward, maintained that the firm had done 'exceptional work' for the government by putting the car business completely on one side, and were therefore entitled to exceptional treatment as regards excess profits tax. Such a claim may now appear, after two wars in which many firms and individuals have done exceptional work without exceptional treatment, somewhat absurd and excessive. But as the following will show there is no doubt that those whose task it was to look at the future from the firm's internal financial point of view could see little prospect for Rolls-Royce after the war. The car business had disappeared. American and British manufacturers who had remained on vehicle work for the government had, in the one case, expanded their output and consolidated home and overseas markets, and in the other increased their productive capacity and maintained their goodwill. The aircraft engine was looked upon as a weapon of war and the scope of civil air transport was not foreseen except by a few whose unorthodox views probably limited their influence.

Despite Johnson's intentions – and it is undeniable that they were sincere – the board fought hard to attain a degree of financial stability by obtaining favourable prices on war contracts. These would permit the firm to weather successfully the uncongenial economic climate of reconversion and provide resources to back its re-entry into the motor-car industry. But those who would seek in these claims grounds for strong criticism should defer their judgement yet awhile.

A letter to the Admiralty on 10 August 1916 set out the amount of capital expenditure involved, the allowance received and the volume of orders required to extinguish the balance. It requested the Admiralty to 'obtain the permission of the Treasury for us to apply Excess Profits (should these be any) to the writing down of capital expenditure'. At a later conference at the Ministry of Munitions on 5 October 1916 the Ministry informed the company that they required all expenditure to be separated, that no decision had been reached on the allowance of £25 per engine as further depreciation and that *some* depreciation might be allowed on plant and buildings. Pre-war rates of depreciation would be applied. The Ministry refused to permit the 1914 and 1915 accounting periods to be amalgamated, and suggested that if Rolls-Royce thought these rates inadequate a valuation of the plant at the conclusion of hostilities would be arranged. For obvious reasons Rolls-Royce wished to avoid such an arrangement.

On 5 March 1917 A. E. Turner, the Director of Contracts in the Air Supplies branch of the Ministry, wrote confirming the conditions which the government were prepared to offer on Tender IV accepted at the end of 1916.[6] The question of excess profits, said Turner, was beyond his control and would have to be taken up with the Ministry. Rolls-Royce refused this offer outright and returned £50,000 of the advance of £100,000 received. On 16 March a conference was held at the Ministry at

which the view was expressed that Rolls-Royce had made an arrangement which no government office ought to have accepted 'inasmuch as
[in De Looze's record of the proceedings] provided the government give
us sufficient orders, we shall obtain tools, and buildings (the latter of a
permanent nature) for nothing, and shall in addition have made
considerable profits out of the goods manufactured therein'.

De Looze stated that Rolls-Royce did not want this additional plant, to
which the Ministry officials replied that it must at least have a scrap
value. De Looze's rejoinder to this was that the country would be
'plastered with works' and the scrap value therefore negligible. The
Ministry representatives then suggested that France and Belgium might
need such plant to assist them to restore the level of industry in
devastated areas, and pointed out finally that if Rolls-Royce adhered to
the £25 per engine arrangement the excess profits department would
'find some way of bleeding' the company. The Ministry was apparently
ready to allow the additional £25 per engine to the contract if
Rolls-Royce on their side would agree that the plant had some residual
value. Thereupon Johnson estimated that the plant, which had in fact
cost £100,000, would have cost £65,000 in peacetime. If the latter figure
were depreciated 15 per cent per annum it would be worth £29,250 in
1920, and on a 'reasonable view' would be worth a maximum of £20,000
to Rolls-Royce. Johnson insisted that De Looze should accept 80 per cent
if necessary but should try for 85 per cent of capital expenditure.

In a letter to Johnson dated 17 March 1917 Claremont summed up his
views on the problem as follows: 'The crux of the problem seems to me to
be the value of the property to us after the war, and that is a very difficult
thing to foresee. With the smallest values we may have to accept that we
may be in a position of having been forced into a very much larger
business than we desire or than is suited for our production.' The
question 'When does a Rolls-Royce cease to be a Rolls-Royce?' had been
one of the constant preoccupations of the management of the company,
and it is a question which has nearly always been considered in the
context of quantity versus quality. Up to a certain point it was believed
that an increase in output would not impair quality, the speed with
which this increase was achieved being of great importance. After this
point it was thought that quality must inevitably decline. There is little
doubt that an equally important consideration has been the character of
the market for the very expensive high-quality product in which a
limited production confers on the article an exclusiveness which gives
its makers a virtual monopoly. If the quantity sold is increased beyond

a certain point, this characteristic may vanish. In this event the firm would find itself in an entirely new market, combining elements of the old and elements of the new and unknown. Radical changes of policy and methods might be required. The quasi-monopolistic position previously enjoyed and carefully, if not consciously, maintained, would almost certainly be impaired. Considerations of this nature were probably in Claremont's mind when he wrote to Johnson; and they have certainly been uppermost in the minds of other executives in a later period of the company's history.

On 18 April 1917 Rolls-Royce attempted to obtain a final settlement from the Ministry, and the solicitors wrote a long and comprehensive letter setting out the firm's point of view.

'The Company with its nominal capital of £200,000 and real capital (pre-war) of about £320,000 was not justified in spending as it has done £350,000 in new buildings and fixed plant. It had no capital and that it had had to borrow any such sum and make any such expenditure was wholly unjustifiable from a business point of view. The expenditure was made merely for war purposes and not for any anticipated development of normal or peacetime business. The only condition on which this company could be expected to make, or which could possibly justify the directors in making, such expenditure, was that orders were forthcoming at a price which would not only yield a suitable rate of profit, but would in the course of two or three years repay the whole or nearly all of the expenditure.'

The letter went on to say that the company 'entertained no sanguine views as to the future utility of the plant in question' due to 'past experience of the economic effect of wars'. It recommended that all buildings and machinery should be written down by 45 per cent, that machinery should be written down by 45 per cent and by 20 per cent per annum from 1 November 1915, and that fixtures should be written down likewise by 45 per cent and 10 per cent and electric installations by 45 per cent and 20 per cent.

The letter concluded with the observation that 'the Company is anxious to emphasise that, as it has done in the past, so in future will it assist the government in every possible way; except that it will not commit itself to any further expenditure of capital which it has not got and cannot obtain by encumbering itself with further heavy loans.' The parting shot was a suggestion that if the Ministry did not approve of these suggestions it should in future lease land from Rolls-Royce and erect its own factories.

The importance of equality of treatment in these types of contracts (an argument used by both sides in negotiations when it suited them) is clearly illustrated by points raised in correspondence between A. W. Claremont (then the company's solicitor and later a director) and a Mr Cooper of the finance branch of the Ministry. In his letter Claremont mentions that it had come to his notice that the Ministry was making some other firm an allowance of 75 per cent depreciation. Cooper replied that this was so, but that the case was exceptional, and that the terms of contracts inevitably became stiffer as the war progressed. 'I think', he said, 'that if you can get a writing down of 45 per cent and 20 per cent per annum afterwards you are not doing too badly. Cannot the Company confidently look forward to many years of increasing activity in respect of aero engines, and does not this Company stand in a very pre-eminent position with the Admiralty in securing orders?' But the company did not share Cooper's confidence in the post-war aero-engine market.

Claude Johnson's comments on this controversy are well summarised in the following extract from a letter written to Claremont on 27 June 1917.

> The rate of profit on articles, the successful design of which is limited to a small number of companies in the world *should* be larger than the rate of profit on an article which is designed and manufactured successfully by a large number of companies all over the world.

Johnson clearly implies that the rate of profit on an article whose manufacture is dependent on exceptional technical skill and ingenuity should be a monopoly profit, though he would not have thought of it as such. The standardisation of profit rates towards which the Ministry was constantly striving in the later stages of the war inevitably bore hardest on firms such as Rolls-Royce which had attained a pre-eminent position through strenuous technical endeavour, skilled administration and farsighted direction of policy, thereby attaining a quasi-monopolistic position for their products which enabled them to earn an above-average rate of profit on either turnover or capital. This they had come to regard as normal. The result of heavy profit taxation was a strenuous endeavour on the part of the managements concerned to secure this real rate of profit – corresponding with their normative concept of what was 'fair' – in some other way. By persuading the Ministry to accept high rates of depreciation on plant and machinery, the real rate of profit would be kept substantially higher than the actual, declared, financial rate, which was subject to the full impact of wartime taxation. If prices were agreed on the basis of accounting costs thus determined, and if these were in fact considerably higher than the real costs (whether the latter were accurately or inaccurately known) the actual profit would be greater than the declared financial profit. Such a process obviously involved considerable risk and the management of Rolls-Royce were aware that this was the case. The process of increasing the real rate of profit by establishing rates of depreciation and obsolescence (the most easily disguised costs) considerably higher than those justified by actual physical deterioration and obsolescence involves the transformation of what would otherwise emerge as cash profits into a combination of fixed and working capital which may or may not be represented by a large depreciation reserve, all available liquid cash and reserves being normally employed in wartime to increase the physical productive capacity of the concern.

Where the basis of the contract price was the ascertained financial cost of previous orders for identical or similar articles, on which an agreed percentage of profit was allowed, lower rates of depreciation would result in lower costs, turnover, gross and net profit. The elements of depreciation caused by actual wear and tear can of course be ascertained with reasonable accuracy, and the limits of disagreement on this component of cost are likely to be fairly narrow. But those elements of cost attributable to obsolescence cannot be determined with scientific accuracy since they depend entirely on the exercise of judgement, at least in an economy where the rate and direction of development generally is determined by independent individual decisions which cannot be predicted. The greater the rapidity of change, always accentuated by war, the greater the justification for a policy of attributing to obsolescence the largest proportion of these costs. In a completely controlled and self-contained economy in which the rate of technological change is determined by a central authority, the problem solves itself. But the price paid for this 'solution' may well be a serious reduction in the overall rate of economic and technological development.

Firms such as Rolls-Royce argued that they alone were in a position to judge the future value of such plant to them, and the State could do little but accept such judgements. A thorough investigation of Rolls-Royce costs had, however, been made for the Admiralty by the accounting firm,

Price Waterhouse. This resulted in a 3.6 per cent reduction in the prices on Tenders III, IV and V. All future contracts were based on these figures, which were adjusted upwards for increased labour and raw material costs. The attitude of the management towards this problem is summed up in a note which De Looze, the secretary, wrote at the time. 'With regard to generous prices', he said, 'the prices for Eagles and Falcons represent a profit of 22 per cent on cost and 17 per cent on invoice value, the latter being the recognised method of calculating profit. We cannot offer to pay for the depreciation out of our 17 per cent – it is absurd.' Officials of the Ministry undoubtedly thought that the Rolls-Royce claims were equally absurd and this controversy shows how easily viewpoints may become as irreconcilable as the personalities involved, where there are no objective criteria or generally accepted standards.

On 7 July 1917 the Director of Aircraft Contracts, A. E. Turner, replied that the suggestion that the government should own all new plant was quite unacceptable. The equipment would be scattered throughout the Rolls-Royce works and would ultimately be quite valueless. Such an arrangement would place the firm in a very strong bargaining position should the government wish to dispose of the plant concerned after the war. Turner therefore suggested that Rolls-Royce should accept provisionally either the rates of 40 per cent on plant and 25 per cent on buildings, subject to review at Rolls-Royce's request one year after the war, or a fixed and final writing off of $33\frac{1}{3}$ per cent on buildings and 45 per cent on plant, with similar terms in both cases for the repair shop. On 13 July the company outlined its objections to this proposal in a lengthy memorandum which objected to interference by a 'new government department' in a procedure of negotiation 'on a mutually satisfactory basis by which the Government agreed to pay Rolls-Royce given amounts towards their capital expenditure'. The memorandum maintained that it was impossible for either the government or Rolls-Royce to foresee whether Rolls-Royce would find it desirable to build aircraft engines on either a large or a small scale. This could be decided, it declared, only if something was known about such imponderables as whether the country would continue to maintain a large air force, how many firms might remain in the aircraft industry, the state of labour and taxation in Great Britain, the extent of tariff protection and the wealth of the population at the end of the war.

Any answers to such questions would have been little more than guesses. The memorandum conceded that the War Cabinet had other preoccupations and concluded that

It is obvious that for Rolls-Royce to spend all or a large proportion of its capital, or to borrow money from the Bank at interest in order to erect more buildings and obtain more plant which it does not know if it will require, would be highly speculative, and would amount to gambling with its capital which might lead to the financial stability of the firm being seriously and irretrievably impaired at the end of the war.

Sir William Weir presided over a conference on the problem at the Ministry on 16 July. Claremont, Basil Johnson (Claude Johnson being in America), De Looze, Wormald (the works manager), Haldenby, and Lomas represented Rolls-Royce. The Ministry officials claimed at once that Rolls-Royce was asking for 100 per cent on capital depreciation, to which Claremont replied that a provisional writing off and post-war valuation came up against the difficulty of who was competent to judge post-war value. Rolls-Royce was not, he declared, prepared 'to spend any further capital which it had not got'. The conference seemed to be getting nowhere when Sir William finally suggested a compromise on the basis of a post-war writing down of 40 per cent on buildings and 50 per cent on machinery and plant up to a total of £450,000 and offered to give his full support to such a scheme.

The proposals were rejected and the conference adjourned. After the others had left Turner discussed the problem with Claremont and told him that when the Admiralty had made their arrangements with Rolls-Royce they were under the impression that the war would be over in six months. In any event, he pointed out, legislation had since appeared which, in effect, cancelled the original arrangements. That the management's hand was finally forced is clear from Claremont's telegram. An agreement was reached, apparently, by appealing to the board on other grounds. On 16 July Turner wrote that in view of the breakdown of the conference the company would no longer be required to proceed with the repair shop.

Under the existing circumstances this would certainly have been a disastrous step. Allied Air Power had recently suffered a series of setbacks in France, and the air raids on London in July had forced the Cabinet to make every possible endeavour to resolve the conflicting views on air policy and to stimulate the output of suitable aircraft and engines at all costs. On 18 July the Ministry was informed that 'in the interests of the nation Rolls-Royce must repair its own engines, and would therefore accept the terms offered as regards past expenditure and the repair shop, but wanted more time before giving a decision on the other contemplated expenditure.' On 24 July Turner replied that the Minister (Lord Cowdray) understood that the expenditure so far incurred was £300,000, a figure which would be increased to £500,000 by the additional expenditure contemplated. Lord Cowdray gave his personal assurance that if the amount allowed to be written off under the various acts was less than 40 per cent on buildings and 50 per cent on plant and machinery, the Ministry would make good the deficiency.

The attacks on London began on 13 June 1917 and continued into July. The Cabinet showed its concern by deciding to increase the output of aero-engines still further to 4500 a month. This would allow squadrons to be equipped for home defence as well as ensuring overwhelming air superiority in France in 1918. General Smuts, who had just arrived in London for the Imperial Conference, was invited to stay on as a member of the War Cabinet and asked to report on the organisation and administration of the whole field of aircraft supply. Lloyd George hoped that Smuts's reputation for independent judgement and impartiality would gain him unanimous support for any recommendations which he might make on a subject which had aroused strong feelings and on which many eminent men had strong views.

Both Lord Cowdray and General Henderson wrote memoranda to Smuts in which they recommended the establishment of an independent Air Ministry, though Lord Cowdray did not think that this would be possible until after the war. Smuts's report was presented on 17 August. He foresaw a great expansion in the use of air power, emphasised its future strategic significance and recommended the immediate formation of an Air Ministry. In a subsequent report dealing specifically with the bombing of London, Smuts attached and endorsed a memorandum by Sir William Weir which stated that the whole organisation of aircraft production would have to be reviewed if the desired output was to be obtained. On 21 September he was asked to head a new committee to be known as the Aerial Operations Committee. This committee almost immediately came to the conclusion that for it to work effectively it would have to decide all priorities, and its name was subsequently changed to the War Priorities Committee. The formation of an Air Ministry was still delayed by the Cabinet but eventually, after Lord Milner had thrown his weight into the contest, Smuts was asked to become Chairman of the Cabinet Air Policy Committee and to draft the bill which set up an Air Ministry. This was introduced on 21 September and became law almost immediately. The Air Council was established and Lord Rothermere became the first Secretary of State for Air with

General Trenchard as Chief of Air Staff. Lord Rothermere was shortly afterwards succeeded by Lord Weir.

These changes in the higher direction of the air war, brought about largely through General Smuts's resolution of the political and inter-service rivalries which had hitherto impeded the creation of an independent ministry, occurred at a time when the 1917 programme was overtaken by one disaster after another. The Sunbeam Arab was a complete failure, only 81 out of an expected 1800 engines having been delivered by the end of 1917. The 200 h.p. Hispano was giving trouble and deliveries were well behind schedule. The B.H.P. was a complete failure from the production point of view, so many modifications being necessary that structural alterations were required in the D.H.4 airframe which had been designed to take it. By the standards of the day, Rolls-Royce engines alone were an unqualified success and a massive expansion programme was at last undertaken. Yet even at this stage the proposals met with considerable opposition. The engine was considered to be complex, and the Ministry had difficulties over repairs. The firm stood out for what it wanted and it was no doubt widely known that the management was critical of government policies and methods. Johnson himself was not reluctant to claim that the Rolls-Royce engines were very specialised pieces of machinery made by specialised methods known only to Rolls-Royce.

Although the attitude of some of the most responsible officials is hardly surprising[7] failure has no great sympathy with success and the achievements of the Derby firm undoubtedly rankled in some quarters. Nevertheless, the charge cannot be laid against Rolls-Royce that the management ever attempted to restrict output for commercial reasons, even if it can be said to have done so for technical reasons. Output was not as great as it might possibly have been because the management refused to achieve this by methods which it considered unsuitable. These methods were tried elsewhere and the correctness of the management's predictions undoubtedly caused great irritation.

But something had to be done to meet the demands of the R.A.F. and, within a few months, a decision was taken to convert the firm from a secondary aero-engine manufacturer to the foremost manufacturer in the United Kingdom. Johnson, as usual, had anticipated the possibility and had already suggested manufacturing Eagles in the United States, from which he cabled on 30 July that he was able to acquire a factory with a potential output of 2000 engines. This was rejected but the eventual decision to manufacture there was to have far-reaching consequences for the firm, if not for the war. It led to the intervention of Rolls-Royce on the American market on a scale which was never contemplated and brought the firm into an entirely new and different economic environment. There are two distinct phases of this development. The first took place during the war. After the war, the company attempted to enter the American luxury car market, but it discovered that selling aero engines to governments in wartime was one thing. Breaking into the U.S. luxury car market was to prove quite another.

6 Failure of a Mission

Jones states in the official British history, *The War in the Air*, that the negotiations for the establishment of a Rolls-Royce factory in America which opened in the middle of 1916 came to nothing chiefly because the British firm was 'unwilling to enter any arrangement which gave them no more than a money interest in the American Company'. Consequently in June 1917 the Air Board contemplated the possibility of 'coercing' Rolls-Royce to come to a reasonable agreement. The Air Board undoubtedly contemplated 'coercion' in June 1917, but there is no trace,[1] on the firm's side, of any negotiations concerning the possibility of manufacture in America until 15 May 1917, when Claude Johnson reported to the board 'having offered to make Rolls-Royce engines for the American Government if it would provide the necessary funds'.[2] Johnson estimated that £750,000 would be required to finance the production of 15–20 Falcons a week. The same board meeting also considered a proposal from Senor C. de Salamanca, the company's Spanish representative, to manufacture aero-engines in Spain. This was turned down, but negotiations, which may have preceded and not followed this meeting, took place between Rolls-Royce and Morgan Grenfell. This company represented the British government in the United States and handled all its American contracts until the arrival of the British War Mission under Lord Northcliffe after America's entry into the war. The position established at this meeting was summed up by Johnson as follows:

> That we are not prepared to enable any company in the United States to make the Rolls-Royce engine because this would necessitate our imparting to them information which would enable them to become serious competitors, not only in the manufacture of aero engines of a design nearly approaching to that of the Rolls-Royce engine, but in the manufacture of a chassis which might compete with the Rolls-Royce chassis.

Rolls-Royce were, he said, prepared to consider two alternative schemes.

The first was to manufacture at a government arsenal under Rolls-Royce supervision 'without the fear of inspection by temporary government officials who hitherto have been and and after war probably will be engaged in the factories of our automobile competitors'. The second was that Rolls-Royce should erect a shop in the United States to assemble parts made by sub-contractors.

The basis of discussion was a programme to spend £350,000 on fixed plant and £400,000 on working capital. During the discussion the Morgan Grenfell representatives suggested to Johnson that conditions in America were such that the only way in which Rolls-Royce engines could be manufactured there was for the company to enter into an alliance with some American firm, an arrangement which would have overcome most of Johnson's objections. They commented adversely on the supply position for American manufacturers who had accepted British orders, and even more adversely on the labour position. Johnson, in his report of the proceedings, commented on this that 'Labour has always been THE difficulty of the American manufacturer – a man can get ten shillings a day for sweeping the streets of New York.'

Johnson suggested Packards as a firm which might be prepared to consider making an engine 'subject to certain conditions', and he envisaged a holding company controlling both concerns. He thought that in view of the fact that Rolls-Royce was unlikely to join the proposed British combination the amalgamation with Packards would place it in a very strong position. Lord Herbert Scott was strongly in favour of such a scheme, but it did not, in Johnson's opinion, offer sufficient safeguards.

The firm's representatives in New York, A. H. Royce, James Royce and S. Nadin, had meanwhile opened negotiations with other firms and with the United States Government. They first interviewed a Mr R. A. Taylor of the Maxwell Motor Company at Dayton, and then a Mr Sanderson of Charles Blainey & Co., who 'did not think it feasible to finance a scheme of this kind except with government aid and guarantee'. But the personal assistant (a Mr Montgomery) to the chairman of the United States Air Production Board, Howard Coffin, had told Sanderson that something had to be done immediately, and Sanderson said that he and a Mr Stone of the American National Company were prepared to go ahead.

The well-known bankers, J. P. Morgan, had acted as purchasing agent for the British government since January 1915 and had established a completely independent organisation under the chairmanship of Mr Stettinius[3] to handle this immense task. When Rolls-Royce representatives called on Mr Stettinius, he told them that J. P. Morgan would not be interested in any private undertaking. He advised them to work in with some other firm which had an established plant and organisation and the backing of the American government, but disliked the idea of an amalgamation with Pierce-Arrow (one of the schemes under consideration) on the grounds that Pierce-Arrow usually wished to control any undertaking with which it amalgamated. Instead he recommended Brewsters, a firm with which Rolls-Royce had already had some dealings, and which was thought to have suitable plant, organisation and backing. The U.S. government had laid down no definite policy on manufacturing plants run by foreign corporations but he did not think that Rolls-Royce would obtain the quality of skilled labour which it needed. The labour market was in a 'deplorable condition' and labour itself 'impossible to control'. For these reasons, Stettinius concluded, neither cars nor aero-engines made by Rolls-Royce in the United States would be successful. He thought that the time 'was most inauspicious for the establishment of new undertakings'.

On 27 June 1917 the Rolls-Royce representatives interviewed Montgomery, who did not share the gloomy if accurate prognostications of Mr Stettinius. He told them that other negotiations with Sunbeams and with a French firm had been unsuccessful and that the matter was urgent. The United States government was prepared to purchase outright one of four plants[4] for the use of Rolls-Royce, and the company's representatives were given four days in which to inspect them and make their choice. Nadin immediately set off on a whirlwind tour and inspected these and several other plants, including the Reliance Works at Lansing, the U.S. Premier Works at Indianapolis, and the Rutlenberger plant at Marion. McLeod of the Aero Production Board also asked him to inspect the Saxon plant in Detroit. Nadin visited all these, a prodigious feat in the days of rail travel, within a few days, and his order of preference placed the Chalmers plant at the head of the list.

On 12 July Johnson reported to the board in London that he had 'so far been unsuccessful in his enquiries with regard to a suitable firm in America with which this Company might amalgamate'. Claremont still remained opposed to any scheme of amalgamation, which he thought 'impracticable by reason of the difficulty of finding a firm which would be sufficiently sympathetic with the Company's methods of administration and its financial policy, which experience had shown required expenditure on a very lavish scale.' He thought that all Rolls-Royce production, apart from temporary measures necessary for the prosecution of the war, should 'emanate from Derby', and hoped that 'no enterprise would be contemplated which would involve entering a highly competitive market' for which he considered Royce and the staff 'quite unsuitable'. At the following board meeting, Johnson announced that he had received cables from Lord Northcliffe and Mr Briggs in the United States and that he thought it imperative that he should go over himself. He suggested that his brother, Basil, should deputise for him in his absence.

He left almost immediately and while in America kept a remarkably complete record of the negotiations which he conducted and the results achieved. Soon after arriving in New York he saw Lord Northcliffe, who told him that the British Empire was 'dependent on the United States for the essentials of war . . . and that no British company could afford to go out for plunder. If the United States demanded, for instance, all facilities for making Rolls-Royce engines, neither the British Government nor Rolls-Royce could refuse.'

Nadin had recommended the Chalmers plant and on 13 July Johnson and Alan Royce had a conference with Montgomery and McLeod and endeavoured to settle a contract. Montgomery was in an expansive mood, expressed delight at the prospect of Rolls-Royce manufacturing in the United States and considered that Rolls-Royce should take over the Chalmers plant 'lock, stock and barrel'. At this stage, however, American law only permitted an order for a maximum of one year's output, which was not to Johnson's liking as the project would tie up a good deal of Rolls-Royce money. He suggested that a second year's profit should be added to the first year's order, to be relinquished if an order for a second year's output was received. Montgomery acceded to this request. Various general heads of agreement were discussed and other differences of opinion soon made themselves apparent. McLeod suggested that it was unlikely that plant depreciation would be allowed as the government would own the plant, to which Johnson replied that an accurate figure for costs must include all real costs, which did not depend on who owned the plant. He pointed out that 'depreciation costs' would make little difference to the total cost of the engine. The discussion ranged next on to the question of labour. McLeod suggested that American labour would make a large difference to costs, but Johnson would not let this pass.

I said that our shop was acknowledged to be second to none in the world for up-to-date tools and methods and that if any argument is seriously to be put forward that a Rolls-Royce workman in a Rolls-

Royce shop does not have as good output with parts of Rolls-Royce engines in one hour as could be produced by any man of any nationality in any shop in the world, I should not be prepared to discuss the question but should have to refer the matter to Lord Northcliffe so that he might take the matter up if he deemed proper with the home authorities. I for one was not prepared to take the responsibility for admitting that my fellow-countrymen working at Derby were less efficient than American workmen.

Claude Johnson was first an Englishman and then a businessman and his intransigent attitude whenever he felt that the question of company prestige was involved probably did much to prejudice the negotiations. Here he evidently confused skill with efficiency, and it was not long before the march of events disproved his assertion. At this stage, Johnson and Royce retired from the conference to formulate the proposals which they later presented.

Johnson stated that he was uncertain whether the Chalmers plant could be converted to manufacture aero-engines and asked for an opportunity to obtain expert advice on this point. He did not view with favour any proposals for the acquisition of plant which involved the purchase of incomplete motor-car or other stock, the completion of such stock while the manufacture of Rolls-Royce engines was proceeding, the possibility of legal complications, the possibility of opposition by a minority of 'outside' shareholders to schemes thought advisable by Rolls-Royce, or the possibility of outside shareholders being represented on the American board. Rolls-Royce was anxious to arrive at a scheme which would allow them to begin manufacturing immediately 'under the direct and unfettered auspices of the United States government', and for these reasons preferred a scheme based on the following proposals. The first was that the United States government should acquire a plant which could be taken over entirely and immediately and rented by Rolls-Royce with an option of purchase over a number of years. The second was that the U.S. government should give Rolls-Royce a firm order for one year's output at cost including all establishment charges and a percentage as Rolls-Royce profits, on the understanding that, if Rolls-Royce received an order for a second year's output, 40 per cent of this figure would represent payment on account of profits for the second year's output. The basis for the second year's output would be cost plus 20 per cent. Finally the U.S. government would make monthly advances on the price of engines sufficient to pay all outgoings.

Johnson also put forward an alternative scheme which was even more unsuited to the climate of American thought. This was that the U.S. government should purchase the works and provide the men, tools, material and sub-contracting facilities, the working capital and a firm order to Rolls-Royce for a quantity of engines. Rolls-Royce would require an option to purchase the plant at a post-war valuation as well as an understanding from the government that Rolls-Royce trade secrets would not be divulged. Rolls-Royce, in their turn, would provide designs and information, control quality, material and methods of manufacture and act as engineers to the U.S. government. Their inspectors would have the right to reject parts, and the firm would receive 20 per cent on the cost of the engines (including all establishment charges, the rent of the works and a sum representing a predetermined rate of depreciation) as remuneration.

Johnson never understated his demands and certainly did not do so on this occasion. There is good reason to suspect that the U.S. officials were somewhat staggered, not only by the general terms which Johnson was offering them, but by the extent to which Rolls-Royce expected the U.S. government to involve itself directly in the aero-engine industry. Johnson misjudged the strength of the hostility shown by American industry towards interference by the state on such a scale and he certainly overestimated the readiness of the administration to assist a foreign firm which could be expected to be in competition with American firms after the war.

On 16 July, Montgomery told Johnson that the government was contemplating acquiring the Maxwell or Chalmers works, and that the Aero Production Board was considering a $40,000,000 contract for Falcons and Eagles, of which sum Rolls-Royce would retain 15 per cent as profit. The government was ready to find the working capital but did not wish to become owner of the plant. Arrangements were consequently being made to discuss various alternative schemes with the owners in New York. The Maxwell Company was aking $1,390,000, and the Chalmers Company $10,000,000 for their plant including stock. Johnson thought the latter price excessive, but he preferred the plant to the Maxwell plant, which would require extra tooling costing over $500,000 to produce an output of 50 engines a week. He thought that if the government succeeded in acquiring the Chalmers plant for Rolls-Royce for $7,500,000 'they should pay us in excess of the 20 per cent on top of cost, a sum per engine which would provide that in the event of our delivering only 5,000 engines the Government will bear three-quarters and Rolls-Royce one-quarter of the cost of the plant.' If 10,000 engines were delivered, Rolls-Royce was prepared to bear half, if 15,000 three-quarters, and if 20,000 the whole of the capital cost. Johnson estimated that there was a reasonable likelihood of a profit of $1250 per engine, which would bring in a total of $6,250,000. He estimated that the Rolls-Royce contribution to the works would be $1,875,000, giving a rate of profit of $1,458,333, or $291,666 per annum for five years.

On the same day a statement was given to Montgomery which maintained that an order for 5000 engines could only be regarded as 25 per cent of the business which would justify Rolls-Royce in spending 7.5 million dollars on the acquisition of the Chalmers plant. It suggested that the U.S. government should therefore bear three-quarters of the cost and pay Rolls-Royce $1125 per engine, providing a total sum of $5,625,000. Johnson added that he did not think that production could begin much before February 1918. Montgomery replied with a counter-proposal suggesting that the government should acquire the plant and place orders with Rolls-Royce for 5000 engines at $8000 apiece, Rolls-Royce receiving 15 per cent on cost to give a total profit of $6,000,000. It seems clear that Montgomery was now playing for time, for within a few days he wrote again saying that his committee had decided to offer Rolls-Royce an order for 1000 engines at 10 per cent on cost. Johnson realised that he had overplayed his hand and that other considerations had determined the Air Production Board's decision not to acquire a large plant for the manufacture of Rolls-Royce engines. There is little doubt that his terms were considered excessive, and he immediately set about pouring oil on troubled waters in an attempt to repair the damage. In his reply to Montgomery he declared that

> In considering these two points, we would ask your Board to bear in mind the fact that we are not here simply to carry out a manufacturing programme, but to bring into the programme the designs and processes of manufacture of sample engines, model parts and exclusive information which are the result of exhaustive experiment and prolonged trials of the severest nature and which will enable us to manufacture an engine which has proved itself to be second to none in war in connection with both naval and army operations.

Johnson never underestimated the actual value of the goodwill of Rolls-Royce, although it was represented by £1 in the balance sheet, but in negotiating with the American government officials, it seems that he misjudged the psychology of his customer. Rolls-Royce was not the only manufacturer of what the American Aeronautics Board considered to be a first-class engine at this time. It was not the only European company negotiating for a licence. The Liberty, for which the most sanguine hopes were entertained, had been designed and tested in a phenomenally short space of time and production on a large scale was started. Moreover the American government would have had to exercise especial care in giving a foreign firm a contract as Johnson demanded. Quite apart from the political and economic considerations there is every indication that Americans, like most other people, tend to show justifiable scepticism towards those who make what they consider to be exaggerated claims for their products.

Undeterred by this setback, Johnson countered with a new set of proposals. He replied that Rolls-Royce would require roughly five million dollars to finance the undertaking. Two million of this was for bonds, half a million for interest, and two-and-a-half million for profit. He suggested that this could be financed by an order for 1600 Falcons at $6800 and 1700 Eagles at $8400. Twenty per cent added to this profit would give a figure of $5,032,000 which, he implied, would have to be free of taxes. Rolls-Royce was prepared to accept a lower percentage of profit if the order was larger.

Nothing came of this offer and in a later interview Johnson attempted to force the issue by telling Montgomery that he intended to cable the board in England in the following terms:

The U.S. government propose that we should acquire plant to make engines for them which will produce a profit only sufficient to pay for this plant and leave us no cash. The order should be completed next July and we have to take our chance of getting further orders. Alternatively, they suggest we should rent plant and they will give us an order which should leave us with a cash profit of between a million and half a million dollars net profit. But after that the government may say 'goodbye' to us. They think they will not but we have to face the risk.

This amounted, in Johnson's opinion, to 'training a works full of men in Rolls-Royce methods and leaving them for some other manufacturer to make aero engines'.

There is no doubt that Johnson's fear that Rolls-Royce's designs and production methods would be disseminated influenced the course of negotiations. The effective mobilisation of industrial resources on this occasion was certainly inhibited. The whole episode illustrates the conflict which must inevitably arise in time of war in a predominantly free-enterprise economy between individuals who seek to protect their commercial interests and those responsible for the ruthless direction of resources demanded by industrial mobilisation. It is a conflict which can never be completely resolved, even in a totalitarian state in which the individual can inflict far greater damage by the mere absence of positive enthusiasm. It has been satisfactorily resolved on the whole in countries such as America and Great Britain because the great majority of decisions are not obstructed by long-term commercial considerations, and because, even where they are so obstructed, any delay and waste is more than amply compensated for by the existence of the positive enthusiasm created by decentralised initiative throughout the industrial system.

Industrial mobilisation would undoubtedly have been more complete and rapid if all firms had banished all consideration of their competitive position at the outset, but this is an ideal which demands a great deal both of private capitalism and of the human nature which it reflects. The capacity to break with tradition is severely limited, even in time of war.

Government officials dealing directly with 'difficult' people such as Johnson would naturally be less favourably disposed towards the divided loyalty which the system inevitably creates. The American Air Board did not approve of such a cable being sent to England, and negotiations continued on the basis of an order for 4000 engines with an allowance of 15 per cent for profit, the government having the right to cancel the order without prejudice to the total profit. The American Air Board pointed out that $7\frac{1}{2}$ per cent of this would be subject to excess profits tax in the United States. On 20 July, the offer was reduced to 2000 Eagles or Falcons (at the Board's choice) of which the first 500 would be Falcons. The rate of profit remained unchanged. The U.S. government was to retain an option on a further 2000 engines, paying Rolls-Royce $7\frac{1}{2}$ per cent if this was not exercised. In this case cost was defined to include any extra capital that Rolls-Royce might have to invest, depreciation of buildings and plant, materials, labour, overheads and all taxes *except* EPT. This contract would, according to Johnson's calculations have provided a profit of $3,060,000 if the option was not exercised and $4,080,000 if 4000 engines were ordered. After deducting plant depreciation and interest the net profit would have been reduced to $940,000 and $1,852,000, $470 per engine (£117) in the first case and $463 (£116) in the second. Johnson was asked to prepare an offer on this basis, but the excess profits provision now proved in its turn to be a stumbling block. Johnson maintained that 'we could not accept terms which left us to bear the burden of EPT without provision in the terms which would enable us to bear the tax.'

Johnson soon realised that he was up against a brick wall and in a letter to Montgomery on 21 July he made another despairing attempt to elucidate the Rolls-Royce point of view. The company had no knowledge of costs and conditions in the United States. It would have to find two-and-a-half million dollars to finance the purchase of the Maxwell plant at Dayton and provide sufficient working capital. This he agreed to do if a whole series of conditions were met.[5]

'We know nothing', he concluded, 'of your EPT therefore we suggest it shall be a condition of the contract that, no matter what deductions may be made by Finance Departments, the profits contemplated shall remain intact.' The tenor of these negotiations provides incontestable evidence that the entrepreneur or investor considers all deductions from the minimum net profit which he regards as normal in a particular risk context to be real costs, and that his calculations and decisions are made on this basis. They can be made on no other if the system is to work. That the Air Production Board considered the excess profits problem insoluble is not surprising, for if they had agreed to Johnson's terms a precedent would have been established which others would have been quick to follow.

On 23 July Johnson wrote a letter to the board in England which indicates that he was under the impression that a firm order for 2000 engines had been placed. In this letter, he asked that everything possible should be done to hasten the departure of the necessary tools and designs from Derby. He had actually telegraphed to Derby for these a fortnight before, but thought it wise not to inform the Production Board that he had done so as he felt it might strengthen their position in the contract negotiations.

Discussion had meanwhile taken place with a Mr Sanderson, the principal creditor of Barneys, a company which in its turn controlled Chalmers. Johnson was somewhat discouraged by the failure of the American production officials to accept his offers with the alacrity which he expected, and cabled the board to this effect. On 23 July the Board replied to his cable as follows:

The Board have considered your dispatch. Your reception is not what they expected from the American Government's official urgent invitation. Results you foreshadowed do not justify the sacrifice of your services here, and failing prompt business the Board recommend your return. You will appreciate that we can only substantially benefit from a sale of goodwill as any profits from trading or acting as advisors or otherwise will be subject to English Excess Profits Tax.

The Excess Profits Tax had a very great influence on policy, both in England and America, and encouraged a quite disproportionate attention to the financial aspects of the situation, holding up many otherwise acceptable plants for urgently required production. The incidence of EPT in the First World War was known to be heavy, but some of this evidence suggests that it may have exercised a serious distorting effect on decisions which affected the optimum allocation of resources in the broad national interest. The futility of losing the war rather than allowing some firms to make what some politicians or officials regarded as 'abnormal' profits did not seem immediately apparent to some of those responsible for supply. In theory the problem should not occur if the state has adequate powers of compulsion. In practice it always does, and neglect of the strongest as opposed to the highest motives in human behaviour, can, as Alfred Marshall once pointed out, defeat the most sensible people in pursuit of the most defensible objectives.

To the board's cable Johnson replied immediately that he had recommended six works in order of merit and that the United States government was now negotiating to acquire one. The terms of the Rolls-Royce contract were being considered by the Advocate General and the Secretary of War. On 25 July Montgomery wrote saying that the Air Production Board had the matter in hand. 'We are awaiting', he said, 'a decision from you as to your views on the several plants mentioned. After you have definitely made up your minds on these points we will consider them here and will take definite action towards acquiring the plant which seems most suitable.' Johnson telegraphed immediately that the Chalmers plant was the most suitable and suggested that Montgomery take 'vigorous action'. Montgomery replied that he was doing so, whereupon Johnson wired Sanderson informing him of their decision. For several days nothing happened while the Rolls-Royce officials waited impatiently for the signal to go ahead.

Unfortunately, a radical change of policy had taken place in Washington, but the Rolls-Royce representatives were not informed of this and were left to guess what had happened when the expected orders failed to materialise. It was probably thought more expedient, in view of the advanced stage which the negotiations had reached, to allow them to continue in the hope that the conditions finally offered would prove unacceptable. The first intimation of what had happened was a telegram on 31 July from Montgomery to Johnson informing him that he was waiting for Chalmers' terms. This was followed by a letter written on 2 August in which Montgomery said 'we have been waiting day by day to hear either from you or Mr. Sanderson in regard to the Chalmers plant', a statement which left Johnson in no doubt whatever as to what had happened. This letter was quite incompatible with Montgomery's earlier statement that the Air Production Board was 'taking definite action towards acquiring the plant', and Johnson wrote immediately to find out what was happening in Washington. His own view was that Montgomery was not prepared to take the necessary steps to acquire the Chalmers plant and he commented in his memorandum that

> Perhaps the manufacturers have not yet learned the lessons which we had to learn at the beginning of the war, namely that in order to serve one's country in a great emergency one must be prepared to make sacrifices. As far as I can recollect the sacrifices which we made resulted in our profits as compared with peace profits being reduced as follows:
>
> | | |
> |------|-----------|
> | 1914 | $100,000 |
> | 1915 | 225,000 |
> | 1916 | 60,000 |

Johnson made his position quite clear in a forceful letter to Montgomery, in which he pointed out that Rolls-Royce were not empowered to negotiate with Chalmers, and that the Air Production Board had given a specific undertaking to acquire the plant which they had not fulfilled. He implied that Rolls-Royce might have been informed in a more forthright and direct manner. Nevertheless, he said, if Montgomery would empower Rolls-Royce to act on behalf of the Allies, he would take immediate steps to acquire the works. This letter presented Montgomery with a clear alternative, and the answer had obviously to come from his superiors who had dictated his line of action.

Johnson was undoubtedly aware of what was going on behind the scenes. He was no fool, and he realised that the amortisation terms which he was asking were exceptional. In a letter to the Board on 24 August, he summed up the main reasons for the failure of the project.

There has been great opposition on the part of American motor manufacturers to the arrangement we have come to with the American Government because they consider that the profits we shall make are altogether excessive. Furthermore the American manufacturers are extremely sore with Rolls-Royce and the Government officials are very sore with Rolls-Royce because the U.S. Government is now in possession of the right to make in America all European aero-engines except Rolls-Royce without paying a royalty. The allied countries may similarly make use of any American designs of which there are none of any proved value.

I have been told by American Government officials who are extremely friendly to us that there is a strong feeling against us in the French Government, in the British Government and in the American Government because we have put our individual interests on a higher plane than the interest of the Allies as a whole and of civilisation in general.

Even American manufacturers, he continued, had very great difficulty in getting contracts and he contrasted the differences in procedure in Washington and London.

The Board must not make the mistake of judging the methods adopted and time occupied out here by the methods adopted and time occupied at home. The relations which exist between the Admiralty and ourselves at home would be absolutely impossible here. No one would believe that an Admiralty official by word of mouth could instruct a manufacturer to proceed with work involving hundreds of thousands of Pounds or that the manufacturer would proceed with it with nothing at all in writing but with the full knowledge of absolute bona fides on the part of both and that a nod would be as good as a contract.

He thought the American offer not ungenerous and suggested that Rolls-Royce would have to accept terms generally accepted by American manufacturers if the firm hoped to obtain any contracts. It is evident from the remainder of this memorandum that Johnson was attempting to influence the board, which had probably prescribed fairly definite limits to the terms of any contract which he might negotiate. These terms were probably not exceptional in England where the unique position of the firm was beginning to be fully appreciated. But in the United States the reputation of Rolls-Royce was still associated with the legend of the Silver Ghost rather than the potentialities of the Eagle. Johnson realised that it would be a great disaster if the world's best aero-engines were not produced in the United States for financial, personal, patriotic or any other reasons. In 1917 many people thought that the war would continue for at least two to three years, and if this had been so it would certainly have been in the interest of the Allies that America should manufacture a proved rather than an unproved engine.

It is my firm belief, [he concluded] that we are not far from the day when it will pay the shareholders of Rolls-Royce to throw the whole of the resources of Rolls-Royce into winning the war and to give up profit-making if profit-making stands in the way of the whole of the resources of the Company being used to win the war . . . This is an axiom with which, I believe, some members of the Board will not agree. The Board should also consider that much of our future business life may lie in this great country . . . We have got to learn to think anew as follows; the winning of the war must be the first consideration in all our actions.

It is to Johnson's great credit that, as will be seen, he followed his own advice. The initial failure, which he probably realised was due as much to the terms he had asked as anything else, did not deter him, and he determined to profit by his mistakes. He pointed out elsewhere in the memorandum that the aero-engine position was serious. Attempts to produce the Hispano-Suiza by Crane-Simplex and Packards had, he thought, failed (though in this he was wrong), and a firm of motor-boat engine makers had also failed to produce the Sunbeam. The Liberty was absorbing all the resources of American design and ingenuity, and Johnson pointed out that all the best factories such as Packards and Cadillac had been reserved for its production. He wished it every success, and later ensured that Rolls-Royce technicians were enabled to contribute very substantially to it.

7 The Pierce-Arrow Merger Proposal

Amalgamation with the American motor-car firm of Pierce-Arrow had already been considered on several occasions previously and the project was revived after Lord Northcliffe, then head of the British Mission in Washington, had heard of the American government's final decision not to produce Rolls-Royce engines. Johnson was encouraged in this direction by the board's reply to his dispatches and cable early in September, which confirmed their general agreement with his policy.

> Board share your jealous regard Company's reputation which is first consideration. Not seeking large profits. Willing make every reasonable sacrifice equitable to shareholders considered necessary to win war. If engines made by others to our design with our assistance suggest 5% and all out of pocket expenses. Board fear amalgamation impracticable but of course would consider favourable proposal as your suggested terms appear to be, subject to proper investigation and valuation and terms as to control etc.

The first official notification of what had happened was received in a letter to Johnson on 28 August from a Mr Deeds, a senior official of the Air Production Board. This informed Johnson that the Board had rejected the proposal mainly on the grounds that no production of aero-engines was likely for at least a year, and that it considered that fifteen to twenty million dollars, the cost of the Rolls-Royce scheme, could be better employed in the Liberty programme. On 28 August Johnson wrote to McLeod of the Air Production Board and placed the whole problem in his hands. He pointed out that the Rolls-Royce mission had come to America originally at the invitation of General Squier,[1] whose letter was couched in such terms that Rolls-Royce could have insisted on the American government fulfilling its obligations. This he had wisely decided not to do. The possibility of manufacturing complete designs was now at an end.

At this stage of the negotiations the British Air Board, which had hitherto been under the impression that Rolls-Royce would be manufacturing for the American government, and had been considering whether or not to take any part of this production not required for the United States forces, cabled Johnson for further details. In a letter written on 31 July Sir William Weir advised Johnson that the Air Board were contemplating the manufacture of Rolls-Royce engines in America, but that he could not commit the Air Board to any definite proposals. He advised Johnson in the meantime to collect information 'as to the possibility of obtaining in America supplies of alloy steels suitable for making stampings and forgings for Rolls-Royce engines, to be used as auxiliary supplies to the Derby Works'. Johnson was asked to have this information ready for Brigadier Cormack who was due to arrive from England to represent the Air Board in Washington.

Johnson still envisaged the possibility of the American government being involved with the Pierce-Arrow amalgamation scheme. The British Military Mission was interested and on 24 August suggested that Pierce-Arrow might manufacture the whole engine. On the 25th, Mr Maurice Olley and Commander Jenkins, a member of Northcliffe's staff, discussed the project with Mr W. Kerr Thomas, a director of Pierce-Arrow, in New York. The latter returned to Buffalo shortly afterwards to discuss it with his board. They considered the proposal on the 30th and another director by the name of Foss had a further discussion with Olley and officials of the Air Production Board in Washington, Johnson having been warned that a British government order would make the acquisition of an American plant much easier.

In a letter to his brother written on 29 August Johnson suggested that the Pierce-Arrow scheme should be pursued whatever happened, but added that he thought that the proposal to manufacture complete engines was 'off the slate'. A cable received on 4 September from Claremont added to the prevailing gloom. This stated that Claremont was endeavouring to induce the British Air Board to provide capital for manufacture in the United States, but that if this did not succeed, Johnson would have to rely on his own resources. Claremont clearly did not wish to amalgamate with an American firm, and suggested that the main object of Johnson's journey was to speed production by procuring manufacturing facilities in America. This Claremont thought he would best be able to do by 'an arrangement with some existing company prepared to make our engines at once and to purchase our American goodwill for cash or shares. If you can make such an arrangement and can quote a price for engines application can be made here for order from Hotel Cecil.'[2]

The negotiations with Pierce-Arrow continued, and on 9 September Johnson reported to the Board that Pierce-Arrow were considering purchasing the right to make Rolls-Royce engines, and informed them that he had suggested 15 per cent on costs as royalty. Cost he defined as 'anything between six and eight thousand dollars', and 15 per cent on this would yield from £180 and £240 profit per engine. A minimum order of 2000 engines was contemplated, which would have brought in from £360,000 to £480,000. Pierce-Arrow costs were estimated to be in the region of $9340 or £1870 per engine and their price in the vicinity of £2200. Johnson suggested that Pierce-Arrow should ask Rolls-Royce to arrange that the United Kingdom government should pay 'such a price for the engine as will enable the American Rolls-Royce Company to grant Pierce-Arrow the right to make the engine and to receive £2000 per engine'. The directors in England would then settle with the British Air Board, acting on behalf of Rolls-Royce Inc. (a company which had just been formed specifically for this purpose), a sum which would be added to Pierce-Arrow's price for the right to use Rolls-Royce designs and information. He emphasised that the board should be careful not to offend American opinion by asking for too much (showing that he was determined not to repeat his earlier mistakes) and reaffirmed his belief that the company's interests in America would be best served by an amalgamation.

At this stage, a lawyer by the name of Kenneth Mackenzie, who had shortly before been appointed the company's legal representative in the United States, appeared on the scene. An astute and energetic individual who was to play a considerable part in the history of the American Company formed after the war, he immediately suggested several further schemes of amalgamation to Johnson. One such scheme was for Pierce-Arrow to enlarge its capital and acquire Rolls-Royce (Pierce-Arrow being by far the larger concern), leaving Rolls-Royce as an independent company with the fact of acquisition not widely known. To do this Mackenzie suggested that Pierce-Arrow should increase its preferred shares by $3,000,000 which would be given to Rolls-Royce in exchange for the tangible assets of the latter, and its ordinary capital by 100,000 shares of no par value representing the remaining intangible assets. The existing capital of Pierce-Arrow consisted of $10,000 in one hundred dollar 8 per cent preference shares which were quoted at par, and 250,000 shares of stock quoted at $38, representing a total market valuation of fourteen million dollars. He suggested the formation of a voting trust which would ensure the continuation of present Rolls-Royce management and methods.

Johnson gave serious consideration to this scheme. He thought that it presented many advantages amongst which he included the elimination of competition by the Pierce-Arrow car, the substitution of the Rolls-Royce aero-engine to be made at Buffalo for possible alternatives, the use by Rolls-Royce of the Pierce-Arrow selling organisation in the United States for all Rolls-Royce products, the reciprocal use by Pierce-Arrow of the Rolls-Royce selling organisation in Europe for the sale of their trucks, and the reciprocal use by Pierce-Arrow owners in England and Rolls-Royce owners in America of Rolls-Royce and Pierce-Arrow service stations. In addition, Rolls-Royce would acquire a new branch of business (the sale of Pierce-Arrow trucks), its shareholders would derive their profits from two works instead of one and the company would be strengthened financially by the enlargement of its asset base.

While Johnson clearly expected Pierce-Arrow to manufacture Rolls-Royce cars instead of their own, they were to continue to produce their own trucks. The other advantages he enumerated would have reduced substantially the joint overheads of both organisations. In later years, Rolls-Royce was to appreciate just how great were the advantages which the company might have obtained from the right to use the Pierce-Arrow selling organisation in the U.S.A. Johnson's farsighted assessment of the potentialities of the American market is amply illustrated by his comment on the aero-engine market.

> Aero engines [he said] must have a great future for commercial use in the United States, the country of long distances, the land where people will embrace and pay for new methods of rapid communication.

Awareness of the economic possibilities opened up by technical advance and achievement is a rare quality. Industrialists who possess the vision, the courage of their convictions, and the power to persuade others to back them, fulfil an indispensable role in an industrial society for which no effective substitute has yet been developed, either within the bureaucracies of European social democracies or the authoritarian structures of more comprehensively controlled societies.

While these somewhat protracted negotiations with Pierce-Arrow were proceeding, the American Secretary of State for War, Newton D. Baker, announced the success of the Liberty engine. In a letter to his brother, Johnson revealed his immediate reaction to this news.

> If Secretary Baker's statements are all proved statements, then the Americans have done a very wonderful thing. Northcliffe said all along about this engine that we must be prepared for the Americans doing things which to us would appear impossible. The success of the engine means a tremendous thing for the Allies; so great that I shall feel no regret at the failure of my mission (in this respect) which I imagine will result.

Shortly after Rolls-Royce officials were told about the results of the Liberty tests on 28 August, Johnson made the interesting discovery that the designers of the Liberty had 'had full access to our drawings and to the drawings of other European engines'. His comment was again characteristic of the man. The military and naval attachés of the American Embassies in Europe would not have been carrying out their duties if 'seeing that we were trying to keep our design secret, they had failed to obtain from Russia, from France, or from England, drawings of our engine'. He immediately offered to assist in any way possible, and requested the permission of the British authorities in Washington to allow the Rolls-Royce experts to design a reduction gearing which the Americans had requested them to do. General Cormack readily assented to this proposal, and replied that he was 'very glad to see that you and the employees of your firm are co-operating so heartily with the United States government, and had great pleasure in informing Lord Northcliffe and Sir Charles Gordon to that effect'. As a result of this arrangement, Maurice Olley was able to make numerous valuable suggestions to Major Vincent, the designer of the Liberty, based on his experience with the Falcon and Eagle.[3]

Despite this setback, the Pierce-Arrow negotiations were not dropped, and Johnson next interviewed a Mr Strauss, a leading director of the company and a member of the banking firm of Seligmans, which was closely associated with Pierce-Arrow. Four somewhat restrictive conditions governed these negotiations: Rolls-Royce policy, property and administration were to remain independent of Pierce-Arrow's control; Rolls-Royce was to continue as an independent company under its own board; there was to be no alteration in Rolls-Royce policy without Rolls-Royce consent; and no restriction on the exchange of information.

Strauss discussed these proposals with the president of Pierce-Arrow (a Mr Clifton), and reached the not unexpected conclusion that what

Rolls-Royce desired in the way of independence was incompatible with what Pierce-Arrow shareholders were entitled to if they bought Rolls-Royce. It is difficult to imagine Johnson himself coming to any other conclusion had the position been reversed. It is most unlikely that he would have agreed to the Pierce-Arrow board having independent control of its policy, property and administration if Rolls-Royce had owned all the shares.

Mackenzie probably realised that Johnson was again attempting to butter his bread on both sides, for he wrote to reassure him that minority stockholders in American companies received fair treatment.

> I believe [he said] that we all agree that the biggest danger in consolidation of a highly successful American company and an equally successful English company is that the probabilities are that one will have been successful through one business policy and the other through another, and that after consolidation this fact may be lost sight of and attempts made to change such policies with disastrous results; and such changes might be made in the utmost good faith but without proper knowledge and appreciation of conditions . . . Fortunately you are in negotiation with one of the very few American companies whose standards and business methods to a large extent approach your own.

The discussions continued but the prospects were not hopeful and on 11 September Johnson cabled home that he feared Pierce-Arrow were not prepared to purchase the Rolls-Royce goodwill in America for shares or cash. The only arrangement which Pierce-Arrow appeared prepared to consider was one under which Rolls-Royce would make a definite agreement with the British government to hand over all designs and technical knowledge to Pierce-Arrow in return for a given royalty per engine. Johnson had in the meantime asked them to supply Washington with a quotation of their price including profit, and he suggested that the Air Board in England should negotiate directly with the American subsidiary which Rolls-Royce had just formed. His views on the subject of amalgamation were as uncompromising as the original proposals might suggest. The only possible arrangement which met with his approval was one 'under which our automobiles and engines would be made by Rolls-Royce, under a Rolls-Royce directorate, are called Rolls-Royce and sold by Rolls-Royce. The difficulty which is always looming up in the background, namely how we are to obtain working capital to operate additional plant after the war, must not be overlooked.'

On 17 September Pierce-Arrow informed Rolls-Royce representatives in Washington that they were not prepared to undertake the manufacture of Rolls-Royce engines, and that the Rolls-Royce terms for amalgamation were unacceptable. Having failed to achieve the impossible Johnson was now prepared to consider the possible, a scheme whereby both actual and theoretical control were given to Pierce-Arrow. As a result of discussions with Mackenzie in particular he had formed the opinion that this would not be abused. 'Personally', he said, 'I should have no hesitation in accepting such an arrangement because I think we should be able to prove to the shareholders of the amalgamated concern, as we were able to prove to Lord Beaverbrook, that the Rolls-Royce business is a peculiar business, that it has been built up by men who control it and who know their business and that interference would probably mean ruination.' This represented a very considerable change in his point of view, but the Pierce-Arrow board were not to know that it had taken place, and there does not appear to have been any attempt to reopen negotiations on that basis. It seems that Johnson accepted the refusal as final, attributing the failure of the negotiations to the timidity of the Pierce-Arrow President, who had founded the company and was now, in his opinion, a drag on its management. In view of the ultimate fate both of the Pierce-Arrow company itself and of the later Rolls-Royce attempts to manufacture cars in the United States after the war, it is interesting to speculate whether such an arrangement would have contributed to the strength of both concerns. The advantages would certainly have been very great, the disadvantages comparatively negligible. Pierce-Arrow would have profited greatly from the very considerable engineering and administrative experience which Rolls-Royce had gained during the war, particularly in the aero-engine field, and Rolls-Royce would have not been tempted into a venture which was to prove a burden and distraction to management throughout the twenties.

In a memorandum written on 20 September Johnson summed up his views on the progress which he had made so far, which was probably a good deal less than the Board had hoped. He emphasised once again his belief in the inevitability of a long war, the importance of shipping as the vital factor limiting the deployment of Allied resources, and the appeal which the more vivid projects such as 'painting the sky black with aeroplanes' made to the American imagination, to the detriment of a more realistic approach. The recent developments of German offensive power might, he thought, persuade people to take the view that the ungeared Liberty engine could not be sufficiently developed to meet the threat. This would be the Eagle's opportunity. He was still determined not to return to England empty-handed.

> Even if the British Government say that Rolls-Royce engines delivered nine months hence do not interest them I shall not leave this country until I have ascertained whether Rolls-Royce engines can be made in the largest number and delivered at the earliest possible date, and until these numbers and dates have been placed before the British Government again, and have been refused by them.

The report concluded with some interesting observations on the Pierce-Arrow organisation. 'They had', he said, 'the right ideas and try to make the best. But the President ought to retire. He is the Pasha of the establishment and his mental attitude permeates throughout the organisation. It is the mental attitude of an old man with one leg in the grave and the other in bed. The idea of undertaking the manufacture of 30 aero-engines a week as well as 200 trucks appalled him, and although his colleagues kept trying to pump vitality into him he kept deflating.' Such are the elements which sometimes, and possibly more often than is generally appreciated, determine policy and influence decisions which many think are based on objective criteria and analysis and result from purely 'economic' forces. If on this occasion both firms failed to equate marginal costs and marginal revenue and to maximise net profit it was for a conglomeration of reasons which find no place in the conventional economics textbook analyses of the problem. These generally underestimate – if indeed they deign to mention – the importance of personality, the defects of organisation and procedure and the clash of value systems.

Johnson concluded his summary with an appraisal of the post-war situation in Britain, where he pointed out that the firm's best customers would be hardest hit by the heavy taxation levied during the war. His old fears, first expressed before the war, were revived by the social and political trends which he had observed and the migratory instinct had been strongly developed by his stay in the United States.

> I do not believe in the future of a business which has only one factory situated in England and which is established principally for the production of a luxury article. I believe that such a business would do well to sacrifice a part of its pride, a part of its imaginary security and

its isolation in order to acquire a stake in an undertaking which has a large factory in a new and enormous country having vast natural resources and an ever-increasing population, and which is engaged in the production and sale of industrial rather than luxury goods. The day when Rolls-Royce could afford to stagger about with a high stomach and a proud look has gone.

This pessimistic prophecy was a little premature, but on his own premise that the war would last until 1920 the argument was fairly sound. Taxation would certainly have reached punitive levels to finance production on the scale which was then projected but which was not actually achieved until the darkest years of the Second World War had passed. But by 1939 the firm had expanded its aero business to such an extent that the manufacture of cars had become virtually an industrial hobby, and it had thus insured, partially by diversity of manufacture, against one of the contingencies which Johnson envisaged. Johnson never underestimated the potentialities of the new industry in which Rolls-Royce found itself fortuitously established by the misfortune of war.

Every remaining possibility of producing engines or parts was explored and in a letter to his brother written on 27 September Johnson mentioned negotiations with a Mr Stearns, whose company had built the Knight engine 'cheaper and more efficiently than it had been built in Coventry', and a conversation with Mr J. B. Duke, the wealthy tobacco magnate. Johnson was under the impression that Duke owned 15,000 Rolls-Royce shares, but his name does not appear directly in the register at this time. Duke thought that Rolls-Royce would be wise 'to have a stake in industrial automobilism in this country' and advised the company not to rely on the luxury automobile. He then proceeded to make what Johnson called the 'astounding suggestion' that Rolls-Royce should combine with Fords. Johnson cannot be accused of a lack of imagination, for having once recovered from the shock he was prepared to admit that 'although at first the suggestion makes one smile, it is clear that if it could be done, such a combination would have wonderful possibilities.[4]

General Cormack had even at this late stage told Johnson that there was still a possibility of the U.S. Navy requiring the Eagle, and by 11 October Johnson had almost concluded an agreement with Stearns when he received a cable informing him that the production of Eagles was not to proceed. He thereupon suggested that Stearns should manufacture the

Falcon, since he was under the impression that the manufacture of the Falcon at Derby had ceased and that jigs and tools were therefore available for this engine. Despite this Commander Jenkins turned the suggestion down.

On 30 September, however, the Rolls-Royce board in England received authority from the Air Board to order parts for 500 Eagles in the United States, and on 1 October the Air Board cabled Johnson to submit to Sir Charles Gordon in Washington 'a complete proposal for the supply of engines under the new circumstances created by the American Government declining to proceed with these engines'. The Air Board was still for some reason under the impression that there was a possibility of Pierce-Arrow making the engines. On 5 October Rolls-Royce cabled Johnson that a promise had been made to the Air Board that if they gave Rolls-Royce suitable assistance in obtaining plant in the United States, Derby would be able to deliver 80 engines per week when the American parts arrived (the existing output being 40 per week). Johnson replied the same day that he understood that the Air Board did not want complete engines made in the United States, and that he was now to organise the manufacture of parts on a considerable scale. To finance this project he estimated that he would need £180,000 and thought it both necessary and wise to register an American company specifically for this purpose. The original order was for parts for 500 engines, but a number of heavy raids on London in October, coupled with the increasingly alarming reports of the production failures of the Sunbeam Arab and other engines, resulted in a Cabinet decision that at least one-third of the 240 squadrons in an expanded Royal Air Force be equipped with Rolls-Royce engines. The decision was made two months too late as far as Johnson was concerned. Most suitable plants in the United States had by this time obtained large contracts from the United States and other governments. Nevertheless, orders for 2000 Eagle engines were received between 20 and 30 October (Tenders 7, 8 and 10), 1500 of which were to be assembled at Derby from parts manufactured in the United States.

At the board meeting on 23 October Basil Johnson reported that in an interview with Sir William Weir the latter had informed him that the British government would probably order 'any number of engines which Rolls-Royce could deliver by the end of November 1918'. Protracted negotiations continued in England over the price to be paid for the English Eagles and those to be manufactured from American parts, but these did not concern Johnson, who proceeded to organise the parts manufacturing programme on an extensive sub-contracting basis in the United States. On 30 November the board authorised eleven inspectors to be sent to America to assist in the purchase of materials. At this time the board was clearly under the impression that the British government had agreed to pay Rolls-Royce £150 profit per engine 'irrespective of cost'. In consequence no time was wasted, as the company stood to gain a net pre-tax profit of £300,000.

The original negotiations for manufacture in America had started in May 1917. The production of parts for the Eagle was finally authorised in November, after months of fruitless and completely wasted effort on Johnson's part, and could not have begun much before January 1918. That the parts manufacture was organised so rapidly and successfully was due solely to the intimate knowledge which Johnson and his small but enthusiastic staff had acquired of the American industrial scene. In the event not one of the 1500 engines made from American parts was completed by 31 December 1918, though production in considerable volume was about to begin when the armistice was signed. This is a most striking example of the importance of speed in wartime decisions affecting industries in which, for obvious technical reasons, several years are required to achieve any significant levels of output.

Fortunately, the Derby production of the Eagle was itself considerable and the engine was not, like so many others, a failure. Had the decision to mass-produce it in the United States been taken in 1916 the resulting increase in Allied air power towards the latter part of 1917 might well have ended the war a good deal sooner.

The total expenditure on the parts programme amounted finally to $9,706,500, of which $9,156,500 was paid out directly by Messrs J.P. Morgan on behalf of the British government, and $549,900 by Rolls-Royce. Three hundred and twenty-seven contracts were placed with a large number of firms, the largest contracts being given to the H.H. Franklin Engineering Company, F.B. Stearns & Co., the Western Machine Products Co. (established specifically to manufacture spares for Rolls-Royce by an independent group), and the Aluminium Castings Co.

From the point of view of both the company and the United Kingdom, this expenditure was a complete waste. The bulk of the materials which were delivered were bought by Rolls-Royce at a scrap valuation in 1920 after prolonged negotiations arising out of the company's own liquidation claims. Had the war continued for a further six months, however, the value of the American components would have been very great.

Thus ended the first stage of the company's American venture. It was, by almost any standards, a fiasco, the story of an excellent idea, which, for reasons obvious from the armchair of the historian, was implemented too late to influence the war in any way. There was one positive gain. The company's representatives in America obtained first-hand experience of American manufacturing methods and conditions, even if they were unable to assess at all accurately the commercial environment of the market which the company shortly attempted to enter. What cannot really be assessed is the effect of keeping the company's most able executive out of England from June 1917 to March 1918, at a time when his services could least be spared. All in all, it was a costly failure, even if its main impact was not on the company's shareholders but on the British taxpayer, who had to foot a massive bill for parts of engines which were never built.

8 The End of the War and Reconversion

Spurred both by the failure of its own production plans and the spread of German air offensive power, the Air Board decided in October 1917, with the full support of the Cabinet, to make every effort to increase the output of Rolls-Royce engines. On 17 December the firm's representatives were invited to attend a conference, presided over by Lord Rothermere, at which Sir Arthur Duckham and Mr Percy Martin were also present. The conference decided not to make Falcon engines in other factories, and to concentrate the entire resources of Derby on increasing output of Eagles. The production of the Falcon, however, was not abandoned entirely and small numbers continued to be produced at Derby until the end of the war.[1] The conference also decided to take over the Clement Talbot works for the repair of Rolls-Royce engines under Rolls-Royce supervision, and this firm started with the easier repair work with the intention of ultimately producing complete engines. In addition the Derby National Shell Factory, one of the many similar co-operative enterprises organised by local initiative in 1915, and the Dudley National Projectile factory were taken over to produce Eagle components under Rolls-Royce direction. The motor-car firm of Wolseley was also considered as an additional Rolls-Royce aero-engine plant, but the project did not materialise. This was due to the opposition both of Vickers and of Basil Johnson, who was loath to introduce Rolls-Royce methods and technique into the factory of an important competitor.

It is significant that the major sub-contracting programme, in the sense which sub-contracting is now understood, and was then understood by Royce and Johnson but by few others, was not initiated until the summer of 1918. When Royce designed the Eagle, he did so specifically with the problem of sub-contracting in mind, and produced an engine whose major sub-assemblies and components could, if necessary, be produced separately and assembled without difficulty. Johnson had already given the Air Board his opinion on the general organisation of sub-contracting throughout the country.

Early in January 1918, Basil Johnson, then deputising for his brother, who was still in America,[2] attended an Air Board conference at which Mr Winston Churchill was present. The output of Rolls-Royce engines was the main item on the agenda. It was suggested at this conference that if the Liberty turned out to be the success which the Americans claimed there might be less need for the Eagle. In such an event, the government would require Rolls-Royce to produce an engine of 600 horsepower which Royce was then engaged in designing. But this was as yet only a gleam in the designer's eye and Basil Johnson was asked to prepare and submit a programme for increasing Eagle output to one hundred a week. Output from 5 January to the beginning of June averaged thirty Eagles and nineteen Falcons per week and did not increase substantially before the war had ended. Yet at this conference it was expected that a figure of one hundred engines per week would be reached in July, and that this would ultimately rise to two hundred and fifty. A new department of the Ministry of Munitions under Sir Alfred Herbert, who had made his name organising the supply of machine tools, was specially established to expedite Rolls-Royce production. It was stated on several occasions by officials at this conference, and clearly understood by the negotiating parties on both sides, that Rolls-Royce was to have full authority to produce as many engines as possible 'without limit' until the Ministry gave notice to the contrary.

The literal interpretation which the Rolls-Royce management undoubtedly gave to these instructions caused grave difficulty when, in the post-war contract liquidation negotiations, the firm attempted to establish the financial responsibility of the Ministry of Munitions for engine production and, in particular, for the associated capital expenditure which Rolls-Royce had incurred. Engine prices increased steadily as the war progressed. The reduction in costs brought about by new methods and increased output was more than overtaken by the rise in wages and raw material costs. Wage increases came about very largely through National Arbitration Tribunal awards affecting the entire industry, or a particular grade of labour throughout an industry, and it is evident that after Rolls-Royce became a controlled establishment, and the responsibility for wage increases had been transferred to the Ministry, the management was not particularly concerned with the consequences, though formal opposition was usually shown by the Employers' Federation. When each successive increase was announced, a calculation was made to discover its effect on the annual wage bill, and calculations of future engine prices were adjusted accordingly.

The effect of contracts in which a government department virtually agrees to underwrite all costs is clearly illustrated by the calculation which is given in detail in Appendix V. This type of calculation was by no means exceptional, either to the firm or other industries where this type of contract was operative. The test of the market is no longer operative and costs become mere indices of physical production. The stimulus of increased profit is largely removed by taxation and only the habit of economy, if strongly developed, remains. Costs cease to be carefully monitored indices of economic efficiency and merely become expenses which have to be recovered. Considerable thought and energy is devoted by the management to this end .There are various substitutes in wartime for the disciplines of the market. These include the habit of economy which it is in the interest of the management to preserve, the availability of comparative costs of other firms making similar or identical products, usually known to government departments and the inspection of accounts and costs by government officials. There is also no doubt that management fears the influence which extravagant and wasteful methods will have on peacetime production methods. Moreover, the absolute scarcity of materials and labour-rationing by quota or allocation imposes disciplines of its own.

The first of these restraints is bound to diminish as the war progresses and a routine of constantly expanding production becomes established. The second is important, but products are rarely identical, and the physical and economic conditions of production even less so. The lowest cost to which the state can point becomes merely a bargaining counter against which firms with higher costs will attempt to set any unfavourable conditions which exist at their own plants – lower intensity of capital equipment, obstructive labour attitudes, discontinuity of production runs due to failure of raw material supply, novelty of product and a variety of extenuating circumstances. The third safeguard would be thought by many to be infallible, but in the First World War its effectiveness over the whole field of production was small. Its influence can never be considerable because of the element of judgement already referred to in connection with the determination of profits. The fourth deterrent is likely to increase in vigour in the face of repeated demands for higher output 'at all costs', and the fifth, though it may well reduce physical waste, might increase other less tangible forms of waste – idle time, waiting for material for example – which are automatically charged to the contract.

This type of contract was not employed extensively outside certain industries where output was vital 'at all costs', but it was invariably applied to Rolls-Royce, and it is significant that by the end of the war the company had supplied more successful aero-engines than any other firm in the country. Its chief merit would seem to be in enabling the management, normally concerned in peacetime with the problems of both production and sale, to devote their attention wholeheartedly to the problems of production alone. Johnson summed the problem up in his remark that in wartime the saving of time rather than money is vital. Obviously the relative importance of time and cost for any particular munition is a problem of logistics requiring the exercise of the most skilled and informed judgement. The phrase and policy of 'at all costs' cannot be applied to *all* munitions. The more widely it is applied the more meaningless it becomes. Moreover, no management can devote its entire attention to production if the financial stability of the firm is thereby endangered and its post-war future placed in jeopardy. But where the financial conditions are such that this can be neglected, the problem of output becomes paramount, and the price which has to be paid is the inevitable waste caused by extravagant methods and by the less easily discernible and often unconscious relaxation of established routines.

A prodigious and successful effort was made to increase output in 1918. Up to the end of 1917, a total of 1480 Eagles and 756 Falcons had been sent to test. In May, the works manager, Wormald, estimated that the total number of engines provided for (in the sense that production arrangements had been made on the basis of firm and prospective orders) amounted to no less than 6100 Eagles and 2075 Falcons, leaving 4620 Eagles and 1319 Falcons still to be made. The 1918 output was estimated at 3000 Eagles and 1319 Falcons. From these figures, Wormald concluded that there would be material in hand at the end of the year for 1620 Eagles and 319 Falcons, unless output exceeded expectations.

At an Air Board conference presided over by Lord Weir on 24 January, engine output was again discussed and it was estimated that the existing programme should raise the peak output to 120 per week by the end of the year or 150 per week with the assistance of outside firms. The Air Board suggested that the Ministry might require as many as 200–250 per week, representing an annual total of 13,000 engines. (The earlier peak output figures give totals of 6240, 7800, 10,400 engines per annum.) The unrealistic nature of those targets, especially in view of the decisions just taken not to produce complete engines in the United States, may be judged from the fact that the lowest figure was twice the output actually achieved.

Ministry officials at this conference agreed that a greater output could be achieved by mass-production based on component and sub-assembly manufacture than by firms attempting to make complete engines. The idea of sub-contractors making parts rather than complete units was very slow in gaining acceptance, but once the decision was taken and the principle understood, a large number of small and medium-sized firms were turned on to Eagle and Falcon parts, to be assembled at Derby or in factories directly under Rolls-Royce control. It was also announced at this conference that Sir Alfred Herbert's staff had taken over from the engine and supply branches of the Air Board all responsibility for Rolls-Royce production. This was a most exceptional situation which finds no parallel elsewhere, and indicates the importance of Rolls-Royce production at this stage of the war. Sir Alfred Herbert's department itself came under the direct control of General Alexander. It was at this conference that the Ministry announced its decision to combine all the recent Rolls-Royce contracts into one large contract, later to be known as Tender XX.

But though the results achieved in 1918 fell short of some of the more fanciful targets, they were none the less substantial. Output improved steadily in the early part of 1918, but it was obvious to the board as early as 28 May that the target of 4100 Eagles would not be reached by the end of the year. The figure of 2700 was considered to be an attainable maximum, and this proved a much more accurate estimate than any made hitherto. It would appear that the Air Board, rather more so than the Rolls-Royce management, misjudged the lag between the decision to increase the rate of output of aero-engines and the achievement of the output required. Still less did there appear to be much understanding of the detailed administrative staff work required to co-ordinate the output of a large number of sub-contractors. The planning of supplies and sub-assemblies remained very much on a hand-to-mouth basis right up to the end of the war, and even when the decision to 'mass-produce' the Eagle was finally taken those responsible were not really aware of the implications of this decision. Nor, as far as it can be ascertained, was there much appreciation of the fact that Derby itself would have been swamped if the output of sub-contractors had exceeded the assembly capacity of the parent factory. Fortunately this did not occur.

The final arrangements between the firm and Ministry were in a very fluid state. No prices were agreed until June, but the Ministry made payments in advance of delivery to enable to company to meet capital expenditure on the understanding that such advances would form a part of the total payment for engines delivered. How great this part was to be was not decided. In addition, the Ministry made periodical payments for work in progress up to 95 per cent of its value, the balance being paid after taking into account advances under the first heading. In March, the Ministry announced that it would in future advance only 20 per cent of the contract prices for work in progress, and 80 per cent of the capital expenditure, 1 per cent interest being charged on both these advances. In the same month, a figure of £135 profit per engine was suggested in reply to the firm's demand for £150. Though the firm's physical assets expanded steadily as the war progressed, the overdraft increased proportionately and by September 1918 it had reached the unprecedented figure of £600,000, creditors accounting for a further £200,000. The board was seriously disturbed by the growth in size of the plant and by the problem of providing working capital to finance reconversion and post-war production. The possibility of either car or aero-engine output on a greater scale than in 1914 was a cause of genuine concern. It was generally believed that any considerable increase in car output would alter fundamentally the character of the company's market, and such a development was considered undesirable both on these grounds and because of the difficulty of obtaining working capital. This problem was discussed continuously at this time and dominated the negotiations with the Ministry.

In June, an attempt was made to consolidate the various Rolls-Royce contracts into the single contract already referred to above. The negotiations opened with a series of proposals by the Ministry, who suggested that instead of the scheme previously employed plant would now be provided at a rental charge, based on cost, of 21 per cent per annum (15 per cent depreciation, 6 per cent interest), Rolls-Royce having an option to purchase at an agreed valuation at the end of the hiring period. Claude Johnson returned from America in March and was authorised by the board to negotiate with the Ministry. He submitted an omnibus tender (Tender XX) which obliged him to seek 'cost plus a reasonable profit, such profits not to be less than the average profits made by the twelve largest aero engine manufacturers working for the Ministry of Munitions'. In its original form, this tender did not include a fixed price, provision being made for both parties to negotiate for an increase or decrease, disagreements being submitted to arbitration. The conditions of payment (an advance of 80 per cent of the capital expenditure on buildings and plant, to be repaid by Rolls-Royce during the period of manufacture, 20 per cent of the total value being a part payment of the price) were much nearer to the old conditions than the new conditions suggested by the Ministry.

The break clause of this contract was most comprehensive. The Ministry could give four months' notice to break the contract, during which period Rolls-Royce could continue to deliver at its normal rate of output. Rolls-Royce could then request the Ministry to purchase all unused material at 5 per cent above its gross cost, and all articles in stock at $7\frac{1}{2}$ per cent above gross cost. The Ministry agreed to indemnify the company against all sub-contractors' claims. Most important was an undertaking that 'we would not be in a worse position as regards the writing off of capital expenditure authorised than we would have been if the contract had not included the break clause.' The company's excess profits duty liability was also to be subject to a 'most-favoured-nation' treatment.

No final agreement was reached at this stage, but the Ministry continued to finance production, both sides apparently content to postpone the final day of reckoning until financial negotiations could be resumed without prejudice to the war effort. On 1 October a further conference on the subject of prices was held at the Ministry at which Sir Philip Henriques (the assistant financial secretary to the Ministry), Mr T.D. Nicol (Controller of Aircraft Contracts) and Claude Johnson were present. Sir Philip maintained that agreement must be reached on some method to keep down costs and increase output and that the Ministry was keen to establish incentives to achieve this end. He suggested that Rolls-Royce and the Ministry should establish a provisional figure for cost and a definite profit per unit of output, any saving on the former being equally divided between the Ministry and the company. Nicol proposed that the Ministry should guarantee the company 6 per cent on turnover at cost as the final basis of the new contract. Neither of these proposals satisfied Johnson and the meeting broke up without having reached agreement.

On 15 October Johnson reported that the turnover for the financial year about to end was £3,000,000, on which the profit before excess profits taxation would be £225,000. Of this amount £150,000 was retainable and he pointed out that a further £100,000 would be absorbed in capital expenditure and £40,000 in taxation. He anticipated that the 1919 turnover would be £4,500,000 and that there would in addition be £3,800,000 of sub-contract work. The government allowance of 6 per cent on the former figure, plus an allowance of £95,000 for sub-contract work, would yield a total profit of £365,000, of which only £185,000 was retainable after EPT. The retainable profit had thus ceased to bear any relation to the volume of turnover, and it is significant that in October two applications for licences to manufacture Rolls-Royce aero-engines, the one from Vickers and the other from France, were declined.

Provisional agreement with the Ministry was reached just before the armistice was signed, the basis of prices for 1918 being the agreed provisional cost of engines and spares, provisional establishment charges at 110 per cent, and $7\frac{1}{2}$ per cent profit on both items, the total to consist of 'ascertained and agreed prices' under all three headings. For the year 1919 the basis was to have been agreed cost and establishment charges, profit being on a sliding scale in accordance with horsepower output, from £50 to £100 for an Eagle built from United Kingdom material and from £50 to £75 for an Eagle built from United States material.

On 11 November, however, the problems of war were overtaken by the problems of peace. Men who had been accustomed for many years to think largely in terms of maximum physical output had to begin the painstaking transition back to the more normal conditions of competitive survival. They discovered that it was far easier to cease fire than to cease production.

The reconversion to car manufacture and the settlement of financial claims against the government was to occupy the best part of two years and although plans for producing cars were put into operation almost immediately the war left a legacy of intractable problems. Aero-engine production continued at peak output for several months to avoid serious labour dislocation and negotiations to liquidate war production contracts continued throughout 1919 and the early part of 1920. The magnitude of the task facing the responsible branch of the Ministry can be gauged from the imprecise nature of the contracts already discussed, and from the fact that throughout the United Kingdom there were 34,000 contracts of a total value of £355 million outstanding when the armistice was signed. Of this total, only £17 million worth were considered to be worth completing.

Though the armistice was unexpected, post-war policy had in fact received considerable attention from the management long before the end of the war. In the transition period management was bound to operate within the limits set by the general demobilisation policy of the government.

The Ministry of Munitions had appointed a committee on demobilisation and reconstruction as early as 1917. This committee considered two alternative policies, the immediate cessation throughout the country of all arms manufacture and the continuation of limited munitions production. It recommended the first alternative on the grounds that, although such a course could cause considerable confusion, it would restore the maximum level of civilian production in the shortest possible time. The Cabinet considered the proposal too drastic, and it was not adopted. Ultimately, instructions were issued to all munitions contractors that there was to be 'no immediate general discharge of munitions workers'. Sir Arthur Duckham took over the liquidation of aircraft and engine contracts and in July 1919 established a special department, the Contracts Liquidation Department, to deal with this work. Throughout the war aircraft and engine manufacturers had been considered an exceptional category because of the novelty and difficulty of their task and the complete disruption of the normal civilian production which this work normally required. It was decided to examine each contract on its merits, and that in assessing claims four factors should be taken into consideration. These were the possible peacetime demand for the wartime product, the extent to which the shops had been specially laid out for war work, the length of time the firm had been engaged on war work, and the peacetime value of materials and semi-manufactured goods in stock at the end of the war.

This policy certainly favoured the aircraft firms and another advantage arose from the decision that aero-engine contracts in general were cheaper to complete than to abandon.

The general production picture at the armistice caused Johnson to indulge in some gloomy forecasts which he based on the following figures:

		Eagles		Falcons
Total ordered		6100		2175
Total delivered	2950		1541	
Total to be delivered	1800		434	
		4750		1975
		1350		200

Thus at the end of the war, 4491 engines had actually been delivered (excluding a small number of Hawks and Renaults) and the Ministry was bound to accept under the break clause a further 2234 engines. Johnson estimated that the Ministry would then have 3120 Eagles in stock, a number sufficient to cover service requirements for over three years. He did not think that civilian requirements would exceed one thousand engines per annum, an optimistic maximum, and suggested that Rolls-Royce should, therefore, take the American Eagle parts over at cost and ask the government to dispose of all Rolls-Royce engines through the firm at a selling commission of 10 per cent. He also wanted a guarantee that the government would not manufacture Rolls-Royce engines or enable other manufacturers to do so.

The total of the original Rolls-Royce claim on the Ministry was £1,451,105, which amounted to a figure of £339 per engine spread over 4279 engines including those delivered and not completely paid for as well as those still to be delivered under the break clause. The invoice price of the cancelled engines amounted to £2,183,000, of which the claim thus represented a proportion of 66.5 per cent. In the calculation of this claim, Johnson makes the following illuminating comment:

It is extremely problematical how the profits accruing during this period under this claim would be dealt with by the revenue department with regard to Excess Profits duty. I am of the opinion that profits accruing under this claim would be subject to duty in the ordinary way. This contingency must therefore be provided for.

There can be no clearer evidence that the entrepreneur tends to regard taxation as a cost of production, a cost which only emerges once profit has been calculated, but a cost nevertheless. The figure of net distributable profit after all taxation has been paid is without doubt the only figure which interested Johnson. If this total (considered as a percentage on either turnover or invested capital) could not be obtained as an open, legitimate and declared financial profit because of the taxation provisions, then it would have to be obtained in some other way, either as a concealed reserve in greatly undervalued stocks, or by obtaining the Ministry's agreement to inflated charges for labour, overheads or depreciation. The reserve in both cases would thus be concealed in a form of physical real investment whose realisation would be extremely difficult other than through a higher rate of peacetime production and consequent net profit. It was clearly a most undesirable alternative from the firm's point of view, as its liquidity was thereby greatly reduced. Any failure to obtain from other sources working capital required to employ the increased volume of real assets left by the war, or a sudden change in the technical or economic environment which rendered the plant or material worthless, might well prove damaging if not disastrous to the whole enterprise.

It is difficult to resist the conclusion that in any firm or industry a given ratio of liquid financial resources to real assets is a necessary precondition of effective action and that this must, in its turn, maintain the ratio within certain limits. Growth, expansion and flexibility all depend on the ratio of liquid resources to the total working capital required, and of that working capital to fixed capital. These ratios will undoubtedly vary for technical and economic reasons from industry to industry and from firm to firm, the limits in the latter case (within any one industry) being considerably narrower than in the former. Whether or not this is a factor which is consciously appreciated by management it is difficult to say. But it seems certain that it is intuitively appreciated. The maintenance of this ratio within these limits is essential to the successful functioning of the enterprise, and therefore ultimately to the continuing emergence of profit, which is but the index of the degree of success achieved in applying a given volume of resources to the attainment of a specific end under given conditions of scarcity.

The Rolls-Royce claim was, of course, contested by the Ministry. Considerable anxiety had been caused by the Ministry's initial attempt to maintain that no contract had been entered into for the 2000 Eagles for whose manufacture the firm had made extensive preparations involving a very considerable sum. Johnson was very indignant over this attitude and immediately arranged for a comprehensive file of correspondence with the Ministry to be printed. This demolished the claim that there was no order because there was no written contract. It also supported his argument that such an attitude was unreasonable and unjustified in view of the tremendous pressure which had been brought to bear upon the firm in 1917/18 to increase output, and the great endeavour which it had made to do so. It was obvious from the correspondence, of which a copy was sent to the Ministry, that the latter's claim would not be upheld in a court of law, and the Ministry eventually agreed not to disregard the 'moral claim' which it now conceded in respect of the 2000 engines.

This brought the settlement no nearer, and negotiations continued without result until the company made a strong protest to the Liquidation of Contracts Committee in July. This at first appeared as if it would effect a settlement, but nothing happened, and at a board meeting in August it was decided to make one more appeal to the committee. If unsuccessful, this would be followed by an appeal to the Lubbock Committee which the government had established specifically for this purpose, and, if this failed, to the Courts. On 2 September a conference was held with General Alexander at which he admitted a total liability of £3,244,000 on the condition that Rolls-Royce would agree to acquire the material concerned (mainly American Eagle parts) at a 'reasonable' price. Johnson alleged that this material was worthless to Rolls-Royce since the Eagle would soon be obsolete. Though it had cost £2,500,000, he considered that it was worth only £176,000 to the company.

The total Rolls-Royce claim had by this time been increased to £2,482,000. If the Ministry agreed, the company would then be entitled to take over most of the spares, unfinished parts and engines and all the American material. General Alexander proposed that all this material should be retained by Rolls-Royce who would receive an outright payment of £1 million in addition. He suggested as an alternative that Rolls-Royce should accept £700,000 and appeal to the Lubbock Committee for the balance of their claim. Neither proposal was accepted, and agreement was not finally reached until 29 January 1920, when a settlement gave Rolls-Royce £935,000 on condition that Eagle engines to the value of £75,000 were completed and delivered to the R.A.F.

This compromise gave the Ministry the best of the bargain. But there is little doubt that the original claim (quite apart from the later claim which was nearly a million larger) was liberally drawn up with a substantial margin inside which concessions could be made, and it is most unlikely that Johnson expected it to be met in full. As it was, the receipt of nearly £1,000,000 in ready cash in January 1920 made it unnecessary for the company to raise fresh capital to continue operations. This settlement absolved the Ministry from all further claims by sub-contractors (other than those in America which were the subject of litigation then proceeding). It did not, however, include claims against the Ministry in respect of capital expenditure.

Johnson's attitude towards this problem is interesting. 'We are dealing', he said, 'with men who very rightly from the taxpayer's point of view, will screw us down to the last farthing. There should be no further negotiation. They should be told to accept our final offer or that negotiations should cease. I am quite aware that the minute of the Board directed me to settle on any reasonable terms, but my feeling is that any further abandonment of our rights would be unreasonable, unjustified and wrong, and that we must bring the fight to an issue.'

One of the bones of contention between the firm and the Ministry was whether or not the material still in America should be brought back, and if so, at whose expense. This Johnson thought to depend on two things – its scrap value in America and the volume of engine orders which Rolls-Royce might still expect to have to fulfil. Over 1000 engines were delivered to the government in 1919, but only eight to civilian customers, so the prospects of the civil market for aero-engines were not very bright. Johnson was hopeful of other developments. 'We must bear in mind that there may be a possibility during the next year of selling a considerable amount of our Eagle stock of material, parts of engines to the Australian Government, also that General Alexander mentioned at our last conference that he understood the Chinese Government were likely to acquire 500 engines instead of 200, and it might be rather sad for us if we received some large orders and had sold a quantity of material in America for scrap.'

This remark demonstrates that Johnson was aware that Rolls-Royce had entered the important new market of Government military orders. Early in November 1919, he asked the Air Ministry what the volume of future orders from this quarter was likely to be. On 26 November he was informed that the Air Council was of the opinion that this would depend entirely on the scale of the peacetime Air Force laid down by Parliament. They were, nevertheless, able to state quite definitely that 'no orders for engines on any considerable scale are contemplated for the next three years and that no deliveries of aeroplanes are likely to be required for at least six months.' Johnson was left to derive such few crumbs of comfort as he could from the concluding statement that it would be necessary from the middle of 1920 onwards to spend £1,000,000 annually to maintain the proposed peace establishments'. The Council also hoped to secure funds for experimental aircraft and engines. The Air Ministry letter concluded:

> On the general question of policy mentioned in your letter the view on the Air Council is that the Government must be prepared to support civil development indirectly by such modest provisions of key aerodromes and shed accommodation at home and on Empire routes as may be found to be required, together with assistance in the way of meteorological information and communications. They are also prepared to consider sympathetically recommendations for the grant, as a temporary measure, of mail studies to approved and established transport lines.

The management cannot have drawn much encouragement from the Air Council's promise to spend £1 million per annum on the entire aircraft industry, and this probably had a great deal to do with the relegation, both by Rolls-Royce and other firms placed equally advantageously, of the aero-engine business to the status of a by-product of motor-car manufacture. This low priority continued until 1931, when state-financed aero-engine orders proved to be one stable element in a very unstable economy.

The dreary process of settling war claims was not completed by the final settlement with the Ministry referred to above. Several large claims had been made against Rolls-Royce by sub-contractors in the United States on the sudden termination of their contracts by the British Purchasing Commission. The most important of these was that of the Western Machine Products Company, whose claim amounted to $428,000 and is not otherwise significant, apart from the light which it throws on the business morality of some mushroom firms of this type. Western Machine Products was set up in 1917 specifically to handle Rolls-Royce contracts, and was financed by a Cleveland bank, one of whose directors was also a director of Western Machine Products. This company had completed a substantial amount of work for Rolls-Royce from whom it had borrowed $100,000 to finance the acquisition of machine tools. When the war ended the Cleveland bank brought pressure to bear on another of its customers, who was financially embarrassed, to purchase the assets of Western Machine Products in order that the latter could meet its obligations to the bank. Just how the bank would profit from such a transaction is not very clear, unless by the transfer of the indebtedness from a bad to a good risk. The customer acted as instructed and purchased the Western Machine Products Company for $325,000. The plant represented an original investment of $436,000, and the directors of Western Machine Products claimed the difference from Rolls-Royce, offsetting against their claim of $40,000 for machine tools. This was the real substance of the claim, which, as was apparently the custom in such cases, was inflated to $428,000 for bargaining purposes.

Rolls-Royce, who had a very much more substantial claim for its machine tools, which Western Machine Products had sold without permission, were advised to put in a counter-claim which was similarly inflated. Rolls-Royce wished for convenience and speed to settle the case, which they would certainly have won, out of court, but Western Machine Products had incurred considerable legal costs and, as the firm had no resources other than its claim on Rolls-Royce, these would not be paid unless the claim was upheld. The attorneys representing Western Machine Products were now virtually in control of the proceedings, and insisted on bringing the case to court. The Rolls-Royce lawyers discovered the real position before the case came up for trial and advised their client to settle for the costs of the Western Machine Products attorneys, the least expensive of three possible courses of action – paying the claim, contesting it, or paying the sum for which the Western Machine Products attorneys would settle out of court. Since Rolls-Royce was merely acting on the Ministry's behalf in this case, the matter was referred back for decision with the result that Rolls-Royce was authorised to make the best settlement possible. Unfortunately for the Western Machine Products attorneys what had been started could not be stopped and the case came up for hearing before the Rolls-Royce attorneys had time to negotiate a settlement. The result of the case was that Rolls-Royce had to pay $22,500 and Western Machine Products all the court costs. This figure bore little relation to either of the original claims or to the justice of the case, for as soon as the hearings began, both parties agreed to this settlement, which probably just equalled the entire bill of the Western Machine Products attorneys.

The settlement of these claims marked the formal completion of the First World War as far as the company was concerned. The problems of peacetime motor-car manufacture now rapidly reasserted themselves. Two decades of peace lay ahead, but it will be profitable before turning attention to the complexities of the twenties to consider briefly the effects of the war on the fortunes and the structure of the company.

The financial information in Appendix VI shows that the company emerged from the war a very much larger organisation than it had been in 1913, and that no immediate contraction of its operations took place in 1919 and 1920. The 1920 turnover and wages figures are in fact greater than those for 1919. The fixed assets of the company expanded very considerably, but their actual value is reflected very conservatively in the balance-sheet figures. The figures for current assets (working capital) and current liabilities could not have increased so substantially without a very much greater increase in the fixed plant of the company. This plant did not turn out to be quite the white elephant which Johnson and others expected it to be.

The years 1914–16 show reduced profits, but this retardation in the rate of increase which had started well before the war did not last long, and the 1917/18 results were sufficiently promising to induce the board to sanction £1 for £1 bonus share issue. This was later regretted. Johnson's absence in America may have had quite a lot to do with this lapse in the cautious dividend and reserve policy of the board.

The plant at Derby had been considerably expanded and the firm was left with a substantial amount of machinery suitable only for aero-engine production. There was really no choice but to continue in this field, but there is every indication that the prospects were regarded with far greater optimism in 1919 than in 1915.

The reputation both of the firm and its products, in the eyes of the public, and of the management and design staff in the eyes of the Air Ministry, stood very high at the end of the war. Rolls-Royce was chosen as one of the four aero-engine firms (the others being Bristols, Napiers and Armstrong-Siddeley) amongst which the government was prepared to distribute such funds as were available. The primary object of this scheme was to ensure independent sources of development work, and to maintain the interest of the motor industry (Bristols being the only firm which had not manufactured cars at some stage of its career) in the aero-engine field. This was in effect a small-scale 'shadow factory scheme' operating within the parent factories.

The company was now firmly established in two quasi-monopolistic markets. The nature of the one has already been discussed. That of the other has already emerged in part, and will do so more fully in a subsequent volume.

There is no doubt that the firm established a secure economic position during the First World War, and in this sense it may be said to have profited from it. The actual profits made from armaments contracts were substantial (especially if the intangible increase in

16. The Vickers Vimy bomber, powered by Rolls-Royce Eagle engines, in which Alcock and Brown made the first east–west crossing of the Atlantic

goodwill is taken into consideration) but they were by no means excessive, either by the pre-war standard which the firm had legitimately established, or by that of other firms which received similar government contracts. The rate of profit on turnover decreased very substantially, though it is of course unlikely that the firm would have achieved this turnover under normal peace conditions. The company made a very significant contribution to the national interest largely because of the obstinate independence of mind of its managing director and his senior executive officials. Their judgement was by no means infallible, but it often displayed unusual originality. On numerous occasions Johnson maintained that the national interest and the interest of the firm were identical, and though it is obviously impossible for any firm to behave in a completely altruistic manner, any wide divergence of national and commercial interest was not welcomed in the sense that some critics of the private-enterprise system might expect it to have been.

The war years took a severe toll of management, as they invariably do. A.H. Briggs and Ernest Claremont, both foundation directors, died within a few months of each other, Briggs in 1920 and Claremont in 1921. Claremont had been chairman of the company since its foundation, and though he is an unobtrusive figure whose activities do not suggest a colourful or robust personality, he must be judged as a chairman by the success of the company over whose fortunes he had presided. He was succeeded by Edward Goulding, on whom a baronetcy and a Privy Councillorship had recently been conferred for political services. Johnson was a very tired man. The war had taken a heavy toll of his restless and creative energy, but he was to remain actively at the helm until 1926, and he did not live to see the failure of the imaginative enterprise which he later launched in the United States. Royce had, of course, worked himself and his staff as hard as ever, and his own health had not improved as a result of four winters in England. The end of the war at least enabled him to return for the winters to Le Canadel, where so much of his best work remained to be done.

The uneasy peace started in a spirit of reasoned hope and high endeavour. Despite its semi-privileged position the Rolls-Royce management did not, as others were tempted to do, sit back and live on their technical and financial capital. In this, the firm was exceptional and British civil and military aviation both had good reason to be grateful to the men who were responsible. One of the main effects of the war was not, however, felt until the thirties. The company's activities were now in fact split into two distinct sections – car and aero-engines. Unfortunately, the latter was regarded as a subsidiary activity, and the management did not realise the full significance of the changes which had taken place and made no attempt at a logical reconstruction of the organisation which this change demanded. Little, if any, development work was done on either the Eagle or the Condor (which was little more than a scaled-up Eagle using a spherical head and having four valves instead of two) in 1919 and 1920. During these years the aero-engine department of Rolls-Royce was occupied mainly in the repair of Eagles and Falcons and the development of the Condor was neglected. This engine, which was developed for the Handley-Page long-range bomber, never saw service during the war. While its development was neglected that of the Napier 'Lion', a fundamentally more modern design, was energetically pursued. It was not until 1921 that the Rolls-Royce management again took a serious interest in aero-engine development at the instigation of Lt.-Col. L. F. R. Fell, then Assistant Director of Engine Design and Research at the Air Ministry, who arranged a production contract for 200 Condors. Rolls-Royce was particularly fortunate, at this stage, in securing the services of A. J. Rowledge, the designer of the 'Lion', as Royce's assistant.

There is some evidence to suggest that the board, because of its failure to appreciate the full significance of the aviation market, received less state support than it might have done for research and developmental work in the immediate aftermath of the war. The company's principal competitors, particularly Napiers, went after and obtained some of the development money which was available from general sources. A very considerable technical lead was very nearly lost and, in this sense, the management can be criticised for living on its capital. But the tradition of virtual dependence on state research and development funding which developed during the Second World War was almost unknown in 1920 and such dependence would have been regarded with some suspicion by the board of a company which regarded itself as one of the pillars of the British free-enterprise system and which sought, after four years of Ministerial control, as complete a recovery as possible of its right to pursue genuinely independent policies.

In 1920, at the last annual general meeting which he addressed, Claremont elaborated at great length on the reasons for the company's success, and in so doing paid a great tribute to Royce and Johnson. He then turned to the problem of organisation, and expressed his belief that the fact that the firm had grown 'layer by layer' was a source of great strength and a cause of great satisfaction to him. 'There is no comparison', he said, 'between its strength and that of a business which suddenly arises like a mushroom in the night. No man living can select the staff for such an organisation at one stroke.' In this final comment, Claremont paid an appropriate tribute to the importance of the human factor in industry.

Appendixes

I FINANCIAL PROGRESS, 1906–14

	Net Worth	Fixed Assets	Current Assets	Current* Liabilities	Net Profit	Additions to Fixed Capital
	£	£	£	£	£	£
1907	109,502	60,079	59,682	14,757	5,390	62,372
1908	114,355	80,506	48,977	19,543	9,063	19,834
1909	137,687	88,933	80,048	33,944	19,994	15,137
1910	184,903	104,027	125,682	44,805	37,760	25,880
1911	216,688	111,920	188,929	84,159	50,713	18,557
1912	373,495	143,882	307,745	78,131	71,062	46,808
1913	421,679	144,794	376,643	99,757	91,183	29,342
1914	414,030	152,776	387,329	106,074	76,850	57,776
					362,015	275,706

* Current liabilities = total liabilities 1907–13. In 1914 a bank mortgage of £20,000 increased this to £126,000.

The above figures are compiled from the published balance sheets which are the only accounts of this period which have survived.

A total of 2976 chassis were produced from the incorporation of the company and this gives a figure of £122 profit per chassis. Turnover figures are not available before 1914.

Appendixes

II TOTAL EXPENDITURE ESTIMATES MADE BY ROLLS-ROYCE ON AERO-ENGINE PRODUCTION IN AUGUST 1916

Tender Number	Total Expenditure undertaken or to be undertaken	Government Repayment	RR are paying	RR are risking
	£	£	£	£
I	100,000	59,375	—	40,625
II	25,000	25,000	—	—
III	125,000	35,000	—	90,000
IV	43,615	16,725	26,890	—
Engine Repair Shop	54,000	27,000	27,000	—
	347,615	163,100	53,890	130,625
Percentage of amount to total expenditure	—	47%	15½%	27½%

Summary of Above Figures

Tender	Buildings	Plant	Total
I	29,000	71,000	100,000
II	—	25,000	25,000
III	34,000	91,000	125,000
IV	26,455	17,160	43,615
Repair Shop	43,000	11,000	54,000
	132,455	215,160	347,615
% of Total	48%	62%	—

III LETTER FROM A.E. TURNER, DIRECTOR OF CONTRACTS, MINISTRY OF MUN-
ITIONS, TO ROLLS-ROYCE SETTING OUT TERMS ON WHICH £100,000 WAS TO
BE ADVANCED

(1) As regards £50,000 for new offices under Tender IV 'the weekly
payments to be made to you under this contract to be limited to 85% of
the value of the work done, the amount of the advance to be recovered
by means of an adjustment towards the end of the contract between
these retentions of 15% and the total sum to be repaid'.
(2) Of the £50,000 required for the repair shop, 'one half of the cost of
the repair shop, not exceeding £25,000, to be a grant by the government, and the balance of the advance for the repair shop to be
recovered by deductions from your bills equivalent to the labour
charges for such repair work during the period of the war; and if any of
this sum is still due from you after the war it shall be repaid by
equivalent recoveries on any other orders for government work placed
with you after the war'.

Advances on account of capital expenditure were laid down on the
following scale:

£ 25 per engine on Tender I
   50 per engine on Tender II
   75 per engine on Tender III
   96 per engine on Tender on 400 engines of Tender IV
   101 per engine on Tender on 300 engines of Tender IV

which left a sum of £75 per engine to be recovered on subsequent
tenders.

IV CONDITIONS PUT FORWARD TO THE U.S. AIR BOARD BY ROLLS-ROYCE IN
1917

(1) A firm order for 2000 engines.
(2) The price to be cost plus 15 per cent.
(3) The U.S. government to have an option for a further 2000 and to
pay $7\frac{1}{2}$ per cent on cost if this was not exercised.
(4) The government to provide the extra plant required and loan the
same free to Rolls-Royce who would have an option to purchase at
an appraised value.

(5) The government to provide weekly sufficient cash to defray 'outgoings'.
(6) Costs to include:

    (a) Interest on capital
    (b) Labour, material and overheads
    (c) State, Federal and Municipal rates and taxes
    (d) Directors' fees
    (e) Depreciation:

Machine Tools	20 per cent
Office furniture	$7\frac{1}{2}$ per cent
Benches	15 per cent
Buildings	10 per cent

(7) All Rolls-Royce plans, designs and processes to remain secret and Rolls-Royce property.
(8) The government to co-operate with Rolls-Royce in procuring labour, material and power.
(9) Profits to be:

    (a) A profit to enable the company to acquire the plant.
    (b) A manufacturer's profit.

V REPRODUCTION OF CALCULATIONS MADE TO ASCERTAIN THE EFFECT OF WAGE AND OTHER COST INCREASES ON AERO-ENGINE PRICES IN 1917

At the end of 1917 altogether 1560 engines were on order and the figure of £123,934 (the total wage increase as calculated below) divided by this number gives a figure of £79   9 11.

Basic wage increase per engine	£79	8 11
Allowance already made in the Price Waterhouse report for increased costs agreed to by the Ministry	50	0 0
	£29	8 11

Agreed Prices	650 *Eagles*	75 *Falcons*
Tender IV	£1550 0 0	£1350 0 0
Tender V		
Add	29 8 11	29 8 11
	£1579 8 11	£1379 8 11

Materials 25% Increase

Eagle Raw Materials £369 @ 25%	92	5	0				
Falcon Raw Materials £314 @ 25%					78	10	0
	£1671	13	11		£1457	18	11

Establishment Charges

Increased by £42,000 17 Aug. award
Increased by   58,000 17 Dec. award

100,000 ÷ 1560	64	2	1		64	2	1
	£1735	16	0		£1522	1	0

Ex-Apprentice Wage increases

£2880 = 1.16. 1 per engine	1	16	1		1	16	1
	£1737	12	1		£1523	17	1

The new prices agreed with the Ministry on 21 December bore a close relation to the above figures.

Eagles 300 Tender III £1745	Falcons Tenders III and IV	
300 Tender IV 1745	600 @ £1470	
250 Tender V 1670		

Calculation of Wage Increase

	Number	17 Aug. award	17 Dec. award	Aug. award Cost p. wk.			Dec. award Cost p. wk.		
Males over 18	3870	3/–	5/–	£ 580	10	0	£ 967	10	0
under 18	623	1/6	2/6	46	14	6	77	17	6
Fem. over 18	1094	2/6		136	15	0			
under 18	384	1/3		24	0	0			
	5971			787	19	6	1045	7	6
		Add 30% overtime		236	7	10	313	12	3
				£1024	7	4	£1358	19	9

£2383   7   1 per week = £123,934 per annum

VI   CHANGES IN FINANCIAL STRUCTURE, 1914–20

Table 1

Year	Net Worth	Fixed Assets	Current Assets	Current Liabilities
1914	£ 414,030	£152,776	£ 387,329	£ 106,074
1915	438,501	180,644[1]	369,036	112,026
1916	500,141	277,242	460,386	237,486
1917	591,198	308,345	1,032,277	749,503
1918	678,459[2]	341,113	2,546,468	2,062,298
1919	1,175,413[3]	337,019	2,465,950	1,708,073
1920	1,220,266	353,482	2,465,950	1,599,164

[1] Including an investment in Automobiles RR France shares valued at £20,000.
[2] Share capital increased by a bonus issue of £200,000 in ordinary shares £1 for £1.
[3] Share capital increased to £787,176 by an issue of £387,176 of ordinary shares.

Table 2

Year	Net Profit	Turnover	Wages	Salaries	Deprec'n	Add's to Fixed Capital
	£	£	£	£	£	£
1914	76,850	627,343	162,268	49,249	9,793	57,776
1915	44,171	501,793	162,299	40,846	12,002	19,904
1916	82,640	1,148,959	342,144	65,355	10,545	107,143
1917	142,056	2,200,963	620,180	127,702	38,259	69,362
1918	153,261	4,289,691	1,223,206	191,978	39,938	72,736
1919	192,777	2,860,530	1,005,042	256,098	50,718	46,843
1920	202,835	3,469,696	1,172,585	269,208	40,585	57,048

The financial year 1918 ended on 31 October.

VII   EXCHANGE OF MEMORANDA AND CABLES BETWEEN THE U.S. EMBASSY
        IN LONDON AND THE U.S. STATE DEPARTMENT

Some cables and correspondence between the American Embassy in
London and the State Department would appear to confirm that the
problem of aero-engine manufacture in the United States was first
seriously considered in May 1917. On 18 May the United States
Naval and Air Attachés attended a meeting of the Air Board in

London at which there took place a long discussion on the general problem of Anglo-American military co-operation in the development and deployment of air strength. The Air Board offered to submit a detailed memorandum suggesting the steps which the United States should take to establish an air service. This report was quickly prepared, and recommended that training machines and high-powered aero-engines should be built in the United States. The engines recommended were the Rolls-Royce, Hispano-Suiza and the Sunbeam.

At the Air Board meeting, in the words of the American Air Attachés report (Major Bolling), 'A great deal of discussion hinged on the question as to whether the Rolls-Royce machine could be manufactured in the United States by existing manufacturers here. I think that the opinion of the experts of the Air Board is to the effect that there are numbers of firms in the U.S. who could manufacture this engine, but it is not an easy thing to do as each engine is more or less a hand-made affair. They stated however that it would be impossible tò send engines to the U.S. or to send skilled mechanics from the Rolls-Royce factory as every engine and every mechanic is needed.'

[U.S. National Archives State Dept. Papers 7112-56]

The original of this meeting was a cable from Colonel Montgomery of the Air Production Board of the Council of National Defense sent to the British Ministry of Munitions through Morgans. This stated that

It is desirable that licence to manufacture in the U.S. be arranged in all cases in the first instance by the British government so that cabled authority by the British government may be sufficient to start manufacture.

This cable stressed the importance of the Pierce-Arrow organisation which Montgomery considered should be kept intact for the purpose of taking on exactly some such task as the production of Rolls-Royce engines.

Meanwhile the Air Production Board and the Joint Army and Navy Technical Board of the United States had been discussing the aero-engine problem, and on 27 May the latter had recommended the production of Clerget and Le Rhône engines. There was from the start a strong prejudice in favour of the French engines, which may have had not a little to do with the ultimate outcome of Johnson's negotiations in America.

A memorandum from Major Bolling to the U.S. Chief of Staff written on 25 May sets out the position quite clearly as regards the British Air Board's view of what should be done in the United States.

> The opinion generally held here, based on statements made by aviation people recently returned from the U.S. is that we have no real conception of the situation as to aeroplane engines; that we think we are producing or in the way to producing, engines suitable for fighting machines; but the view held by aviation experts here is that . . . our engines are suitable for training purposes, and for training purposes only; so that we have a long road to go before we can get an engine suitable for fighting purposes.
>
> [State Dept. 7112-61]

That Johnson was likely to meet with considerable difficulty in persuading the U.S. authorities to build the Rolls-Royce aero-engine can also be judged from the fact that on 1 June, Major William Mitchell, then Air Attaché to the French Government, had cabled the Chief of Staff in Washington that he favoured the British tactical formations in the air and the French engines. 'To have successful motors the Lorraine-Dietrich, Le Rhône, Clerget and Hispano-Suiza must be used and arrangements made for their production at once to insure their fabrication by next summer.'

[State Dept. 7112-58]

On 29 June the American Ambassador in London cabled the U.S. Secretary of State that it was 'absolutely necessary that big production of Hispano-Suiza motors be started immediately' and also advised him to expedite the deliveries of Curtis engines. It is obvious from these documents that the engine problem was causing great concern, but two further dispatches reveal that the choice of the Rolls-Royce was being prejudiced by commercial considerations of a type very similar to those which hindered Johnson's negotiations in the United States in July and August. Two further cables reveal that the authorities were very averse to the payment of royalties. The first of these, from Major Bolling to General Squier of the Air Production

Board, expressly requested the latter not to negotiate on a royalty basis.

Yours 27th re royalties. It is essential that no arrangement be made by you with private firms pending conclusion our negotiations. British military authorities have indicated approval of our position. Any arrangements with private parties will cause serious difficulties here.

[Ibid., 102/2.506]

Air Board opinion is that Clerget 130 and Le Rhône 110 both unsatisfactory, though Le Rhône much better than Clerget. Both services have accepted 140–150 AR 1 Rotary on which no royalties are demanded.

[Ibid., 102/2.506]

The importance of the payment of royalties, of the cost of the engine rather than the quality as a prime consideration is all too obvious from the latter of the above two cables. The first dispatch, however, reveals that the problem was causing concern at the very highest level. The American Ambassador, Mr Page, was a strong advocate of air power, and earlier dispatches show that he was conscious of the importance of not disrupting the supplies from the United States to the Allies while the former armed. On the subject of manufacturing rights he cabled the State Department on 2 July as follows:

Regarding payments for British rights, matter has very important industrial, political and diplomatic aspects. Question much larger than first appeared. Military members of Air Board hold views mentioned my cables eight and seventeen. Civilian members coming assist immediate start our programme by removing all difficulties regarding rights, but they recognise great importance matter assumes here. It will probably be submitted to Prime Minister and Cabinet but I think progress favourable, meanwhile airplanes, engines, drawings etc., will be sent out immediately under promise we will not use them until agreement is reached. Appear necessary that I proceed Paris at once to take up negotiations there while matter is considered here. . . .

[102.2/54]

This was followed on the same day by a further cable suggesting the possibility of manufacturing the Sunbeam.

British state Willys manufacturing in America parts for Sunbeam's copy and improvement Hispano-Suiza. Assembly is in Canada. Willys has order for 1,000 of these engines, delivery about 100 per month beginning in October. Suggest you investigate thoroughly and rapidly possibilities for building this engine in large quantities in the United States, said to be absolutely interchangeable with Hispano-Suiza . . . Plans for building should be arranged immediately so as to commence immediately in case decision by production board.

The Eagle was by no means the only pebble on the beach at this stage of the negotiations, and the following dispatch from the Air Attaché, Major Bolling, to General Squier and Howard Coffin of the Air Board reveals that the Rolls-Royce officials had already created quite a reputation for themselves. It left the Air Board in no doubt as to what was considered to be the best engine.

Everyone here agrees Rolls-Royce most dependable high-power engine and essential for use large sea-planes but all say it is impossible for quantity production and think great quantity engines almost as good is more important. Big British air programme contemplates only 10% of big engines Rolls-Royce simply because they consider no more can be produced. Our engine experts agree with these conclusions. Air Board and ourselves recommend that you do *not* include Rolls-Royce in our programme quantity production but that Rolls-Royce people be encouraged to conclude their negotiations with Pierce-Arrow for their factory in America for which British and ourselves will take all engines that can be produced. If our views are correct this will secure as large output as can be secured anyhow. All agree Rolls-Royce people most difficult to deal with. Reported here Duke of American Tobacco Company chief owner Rolls-Royce. Advise enquiry.

[522 MF]

These cables reveal that there was a widespread prejudice against the Rolls-Royce engines because of their alleged complexity, and against the company because of the intransigence of its officials. In the light of the above interchange of cables it is not altogether surprising that Johnson did not succeed in his mission.

Notes

1. From a private memorandum written for Claude Johnson, 21 June 1923.
2. His main work in Liverpool was on theatre lighting, still a very primitive affair. Royce considered one of the main advantages of this work to be the opportunity which it afforded him of seeing most of the shows free.
3. Royce's first vehicle was not a car at all but a De Dion 'Quad', a four-wheeled bicycle whose uncertain and erratic behaviour irritated a man of his temperament. The rockery at his Knutsford house was deliberately sited at the end of the drive to act as a buffer in the event of brake failure.
4. The output of motor cars in France was as follows:

Year	Number	Total value (£)	Export value (£)
1898	1,850	320,000	69,970
1899	1,900	367,000	170,372
1900	5,000	1,062,000	376,660
1901	8,800	2,046,000	631,260
1902	16,500	3,821,000	1,209,240
1903	19,500	5,250,000	2,033,480
1904 (est.)	22,000	6,800,000	2,841,400

5. *Motor Trader*, 1906.
6. According to Edge these firms were the following: Argyll, Humber, Wolseley, Daimler, Rober, Napier.
7. *Autocar*.
8. An interesting technical comparison of the Decauville 10 h.p. and the first Royce 10 h.p. cars has since been published in *The Rolls-Royce Owner*, Vol. I, No. 7.
9. I am indebted to Ernest Wooler, who was living in the U.S.A. in 1948 and had by then retired and become Mayor of Pompano, Florida, for the following vivid description of his apprenticeship to Henry Royce in 1903, a qualification which, he believes, entitles him to claim to be the first premium apprentice in the British motor-car industry. This qualification is one which, he has said, he 'wouldn't trade for all the colleges in the U.S.A.'.

Royce, Claremont and De Looze often visited our home when I was a child so it was only natural I became the first premium apprentice in the motor-car industry in 1903 at 6/- a week, if I was on time, 6.00 a.m. till 5.30 p.m., and lots of overtime for and with Mr. Royce, at 2d per hour. After we got the sketches of the Decauville car they were used by the draughtsmen, two 'experienced' auto designers, Adams and Shipley, to design the Royce 2 cyl. car. But "Old man Royce" did the designing . . . every little detail. I personally traced, made blueprints, ran errands, small details, all calculated out and each and every one with Royce's mechanical genius standing out all over it. The radiator design, not for beauty but mechanically correct which gave it mechanical beauty and class etc. etc. I helped assemble the first car and Royce worked right along with us in overalls at times. He wanted a leather washer or gasket one day – or rather night. Nothing in the stock room was suitable or at least I could not find anything. Impatiently he tore off one of his leather leggings he wore occasionally in those days and threw it at me to "make it out of that quickly". He sometimes came to the works with only one legging on, or without a tie. Motor cars on his mind all the time . . . Royce's personal interest in everyone's work was very gratifying. He'd rush through his electrical work to get on to his plaything – as we thought the Royce car, especially in the Drawing office, much to the disgust of the electrical department and the delight of the few favoured ones on motor-car work.

We sure missed Mr. Royce when we went to Derby. He never came down while we were building the works and very little afterwards. He was too busy and interested in the engineering in Manchester.

My favourite story of RR workmanship – design and quality to Americans when they ask me about it, as they often do, is the use of taper bolts instead of rivets. I remember Royce carefully explaining to me as a child how a hot rivet never filled a hole when it cooled. A cold rivet was punishing the metal too much. So we made taper bolts fitted perfectly in a hand-reamed hole. It is such details that explain the difference between Rolls-Royce and other cars and Rolls-Royce quality. Also Royce himself, who taught us all the principles which carried on in the whole organisation.

[Extracts from a letter to the author in 1948]

10. Royce gave the following estimates of the cost of this car:

		£		
Frame and fittings		£ 19	11	2
Engine		32	13	2
Rear axle		22	1	1
Front axle		13	5	10
Gear box		11	10	11½
Other items		38	11	10
		£138	3	0½

This does not suggest a very expensive vehicle, but the estimate presumably takes no account of Royce's own time.

11. Four types were advertised by Rolls:

10 h.p. Tonneau 4-seater	£395
10 h.p. Park Phaeton 2-seater	£436
30 h.p. 6-cyl. Tonneau, Limousine	£890 and £1000
15 h.p. 3-cyl. Landaulet	£500

All were fitted with Barker bodies.

12. Estimates of production costs at the new factory:

	1	2	3
Chassis	1,000	500	300
Bodies and chassis*	800	400	240
Cost of chassis alone	387,000	193,500	—
Chassis and bodies	381,600	190,800	—
Men required	1,040	520	—

Men = 250 per acre; Acres £2 per square yard. Incidentals 20%.

4 acres	19,360	
2 acres	9,680	
1 acre	5,808	

	1	2	3
Land	38,720	23,332	13,939
Equipment			
Machine men at £200 each incl. all tools and accessories	580	290	174
Fitters @ £20 each incidentals 20%	460	230	138
	137,720	68,860	41,316
Stock in trade and work in progress not allowing for any complete cars kept in stock	98,000	49,000	29,400
	282,184	141,092	84,655

* Royce Ltd manufactured no bodies.

13. Johnson also mentions the Doxfords, Moreland (a successful match manufacturer in Manchester, Hornby Lewis, Leicester Harmsworth and Sir Wellington Avery, the last two both being interested in Darracqs, which he thought might be a disadvantage.

CHAPTER 2

1.

	Stretford			Bradford			Leicester			Coventry		
Power	1425	0	0	1406	8	0	1250	0	0	1281	0	0
Rates on Buildings and Machinery	63 15 226	0 13	4	422	16	3	186	3	5	128	3	2
Buildings	6000	0	0	5000	0	0	5000	0	0	5000	0	0
							(No building restriction, need only take 2 acres then will hold any quantity up to 4 for 5 years)					
Land 4 acres Rent	282	6	8	201	13	4	60	0	0	96	0	0
Labour Road-making	1600 500	0 0	0 0	Something at Mr Briggs' end			None			500	0	0
Carriage 200 tons raw material	1076	13	4	1190	0	0	887	10	0	958	6	8
	4674	8	4	3220	14	7	2383	13	5	2463	14	10

body-making can only be considered at Leicester and Coventry.

2. Quite apart from the decision to standardise, the choice on Royce's part of the six-cylinder engine took considerable courage. The cylinder controversy was at its height, and Royce had only just succeeded in producing the first smooth six-cylinder engine (free from torsion vibrations of the crankshaft) after a series of experiments with hardwood centred flywheels. This work anticipated that of Lanchester by several months, but Royce had not patented and Lanchester threatened to sue for infringement. Royce instructed the drawing office to send him dated photographs and drawings and nothing more was heard on the subject. Lanchester's patent was in any case too loosely worded for him to have been able to gain any real protection from it.

3. The following table of profits illustrates the precarious condition of several major companies in the industry at this time:

	1904	1905	1906	1907	1908	
Rover	£−1,769	16,211	16,116	16,870	− 5,388	
Humber	1,125	6,537	106,559	154,434	−23,499	Loss
Daimler	—	83,167	213,000	124,213	−49,286	

4. On many occasions, both during Royce's lifetime and subsequently, the shortage of key technical and administrative staff prevented the Company from entering new and possibly very profitable fields or from expanding production. This, and not shortage of capital or skilled labour, has

invariably been the limiting factor. It is the type of skill, judgement or ability which cannot be trained in a few months that cannot readily be multiplied, and it is both difficult, and generally uneconomical, to maintain large reserves of such men, which becomes particularly critical in wartime.

5. See Chapter 3, 'Consolidation and Expansion', Page 36.

CHAPTER 3

1. It was only relatively recently that the significant cost reductions achieved through quantity production have been fully appreciated in Rolls-Royce. These economies are proportionately far greater for an increase of output from two to four thousand cars per annum than they are for an increase of two hundred thousand to four hundred thousand cars per annum. A firm like Rolls-Royce operates on the steepest portion of the average cost curve, Ford on the flattest. It is, of course, arguable, as Philip Andrews pointed out to me, that were a company such as Ford to produce the Rolls-Royce product, their cost curve, over the same range, would be much steeper than Rolls-Royce's, since entirely different mass-production methods would offer substantial economies much more quickly. But as far as can be seen, the management of Rolls-Royce never considered their demand curve as elastic. The disadvantages of quantity output have always been thought of as far more dangerous than any reduction in costs which this might achieve.

2. The second largest holding was that of Lord Llangattock who had taken over Rolls's holding on his death. This amounted to 26,500 shares.

3. A block of 10,000 shares was divided amongst 22 individuals and companies of which one was the Canadian Empire Investment Trust, operating from 75 Lombard Street.

4. Later Lord Wargrave, chairman of the board from 1923 to 1936.

CHAPTER 4

1. Ministry of Munitions, *Official History.*

2. See Claude Johnson's memorandum to the Air Board, p. 71.

3. Raleigh and Jones, *The War in the Air*, Vol. VI.

4. I am indebted to Mr Maurice Olley for the following interesting details of Royce's final conversion to the idea of designing and manufacturing an aero-engine for the Allies. Royce, a friend by the name of Randall, and Maurice Olley were sitting in his garden at St Margaret's Bay (near Dover) watching a blimp carrying dispatches from France struggling to make its way against a strong headwind. The airship was almost stationary and Randall suggested to Royce that he was sure that a Silver Ghost car engine could do much better if only Royce would agree to install it. Both of them did their utmost to persuade Royce that he should not only modify the Silver Ghost engine but that he should design a first-class aero-engine for the British Government. He even-

tually agreed to do so and immediately set to work studying the details of what was the best German aero-engine then in existence, the Mercedes-Benz. He considered that Britain would do far better by taking advantage of all the work that the Germans had done than by starting from scratch on an entirely new type of engine. The basic design of the Eagle, which was the first actual aero-engine that Royce designed was thus based on the Mercedes-Benz but it was substantially different in detail and in due course was developed by Royce into a greatly superior engine.

This design was taken to Mervyn O'Gorman at the R.A.E. but the latter was not impressed. He considered that the output of 200 h.p. was too great and that the engine would only be useful in a twin-engined bomber. He also argued that it would have to be set transversely in an airframe or airship frame and that it should not on this account exceed forty-eight inches in length. At this stage of its existence the R.A.E. was a strong protagonist of air-cooled engines for aircraft. Air-cooled engines were considered to be a logical method of propelling 'air'-craft and the R.A.E. would not accept Royce's argument that this type of engine required a great deal of development and that there was no intrinsic reason why a liquid-cooled engine should not be used. The first interviews with the R.A.E. were not very satisfactory in consequence. Royce considered that their views were very inflexible and he determined to forge ahead on his own. However, the design was enthusiastically supported by Commander Briggs, to whom it was shown next, and on Brigg's recommendation Johnson agreed to support the development of the engine financially from the firm's own resources in its early stages.

5. Johnson had been attempting to obtain a contract for machine guns almost continuously from the outbreak of war. He foresaw the need for them a good deal more clearly than those responsible at the War Office. It is equally remarkable that in the Second World War Rolls-Royce (in the person of its managing director) should similarly have foreseen the need for anti-tank cannon on aircraft long before this was generally appreciated in military circles.

6. The following are the conditions of manufacture which Rolls-Royce laid down:

   (a) The Government would provide £93,000 for the purpose of building and equipping a factory. This sum would be repayable at the rate of £15 per rifle delivered and Rolls-Royce would pay 5 per cent on the amount outstanding. When an amount of £69,750 had been repaid the factory and its contents would become the property of the company.

   (b) The government would provide £75,000, the estimated working capital required to produce 5000 rifles, and an advance on account of purchase price payable of £10,000, the figure demanded by the Copenhagen syndicate. Rolls-Royce would pay 5 per cent p.a. on this total, which would be repaid at the rate of £33 6 8 per rifle delivered.

   (c) The profit would be divided between Rolls-Royce and the syndicate on the ratio of $\frac{3}{5}$ths to $\frac{2}{5}$ths.

(d) Under certain circumstances the government was to have the right to reduce the order to 2000 rifles and various terms of reduction and cancellation were agreed.

7. The chief engineer of this company was A.H.R. Fedden, later Sir Roy Fedden, and it is significant that this concern, under the name of the Cosmo Engineering Company which it adopted after the war, was bought up by the Bristol Aeroplane Company and became the foundation of the aero-engine division of Bristols, Rolls-Royce's principal competitor in this field in the inter-war years.

8.

300 Eagles @ £1300 each	£390,000
375 Falcons @ £1100 each	412,500
100 Hawks @ £630 each	63,000
	£865,500

9. The real reason for most of this trouble was the department's policy of encouraging sub-contracting firms to make complete engines instead of concentrating on parts to increase the output of the parent factory. It led inevitably to a great drain on the technical resources of the parent factory.

10. To some extent the argument of lack of interchangeability was exaggerated for the purpose of supporting the firm's case that it should control repair work. Rolls-Royce aircraft engine parts were in fact far more nearly interchangeable than most parts of so-called precision manufactured aero-engines in production at this time. The whole design of Rolls-Royce engines, which were assemblies of nominally interchangeable sub-assemblies, was specifically adapted for repair in depots.

11. Parliamentary Committee of Investigation into Aero-engine Production, Cmd 8194.

12. *History of the Ministry of Munitions*, Vol. XII, Section 1, 'Aero Supplies: 'It was considered impossible to duplicate the specialised labour employed by the Derby firm for the purpose of using other contractors on Rolls-Royce design; nor was the co-operation of the contractors very satisfactory. There was also the undoubted fact that the Rolls-Royce firm did not view with enthusiasm the handing over of their designs to other firms for their manufacture, particularly to other firms in the United States. They were not only extremely jealous of their production but also of their good name which, it was anticipated, might suffer in the event of another firm turning out an inferior model of their design. At this time this outlook was regarded by many as an obstructionist attitude.'

13. This remark referred presumably to the practice of private firms submitting their engine designs to Farnborough designers for approval before government orders were given.

CHAPTER 5

1. The anticipated delivery schedule in 1915 for these engines was as follows:

   Eagles – 15 per week commencing early in February
   Hawks – 27 per month in March and April, 24 in May
   Falcons – March 24   July   80
            April 24   August   66
            May   24   September 56
            June 76   October   25

2. The Hispano factory was erected at Clichy at a cost of 75 million francs, and was run on behalf of the British government by a firm of American bankers by the name of Thorne. After the war, Rolls-Royce contemplated leasing a section of this factory but the negotiations came to nothing.
3. Memo to Imperial Defence Committee – J.C. Nerney.
4. Royce was working at this time at West Wittering, where his design headquarters was to remain for the rest of his life, and a fortunate result of this arrangement is that most of his ideas were put down on paper to be sent up to Derby. In one of the first of these memos which has survived (R.1/B.12.5.17) Royce commented on the controversy mentioned above: 'I think it would be a mistake for us to drop the Falcon engine. I would much rather drop the Eagle. The Falcon will be doing 270 b.h.p. and possibly up to 300 and will be a big powered engine and can possibly be lightened. There is more risk, I think, of our being told to slow down if we were manufacturing Eagles than if we were manufacturing Falcons. I do not believe the Air Board have yet got a good engine of about 250 b.h.p. which is free from vibration, as is the case with all the eight-cylinder engines. We understand the geared Hispano is not a success.'
5. See Appendix II.
6. See Appendix III.
7. At a Ministry conference on 11 November 1917 Sir William Weir made the following statement:

   Mr. Martin and I are firmly of the opinion that, in view of other designs of engines, better results can be obtained by training existing works and establishing new works to build designs other than the Rolls-Royce, especially when time and quantity are of important consideration.

   Sir Arthur Duckham stated: 'I do not consider we should increase the production of complicated types.'
                              History of the Ministry of Munitions, Vol. XII.

CHAPTER 6

1. At an Air Board meeting in June General Henderson had asked if Rolls-Royce could be commandeered. Mr Percy Martin replied that 'while it might be possible to commandeer the Rolls-Royce engines it was not possible to commandeer a capable staff to carry on their manufacture in the United States' and stated that he did not like the idea of commandeering a British firm in the interests of a foreign government.
2. See Appendix VII.
3. Administrator of the Lend-Lease programme during the Second World War.
4. Locomobile, Chalmers, Maxwell and Brewsters.
5. The conditions are set out in detail in Appendix IV.

CHAPTER 7

1. Johnson maintained elsewhere that the original invitation was the result of pressure by a group on the Air Production Board which wished to have an engine in reserve in case the Liberty proved a failure. This group was outvoted when it seemed certain that the Liberty, which ran its first test in July, would prove a success.
2. Hotel Cecil – London headquarters of the Air Board.
3. This offer of help was no idle formality. The British Aeronautical Mission to America reported as follows:

   It should be clearly noted that the design of this gear [reduction gear of the epicyclic-geared engine] has been carried out in the main by Messrs. Rolls-Royce representatives for the Aircraft Production Bureau and it is considered that some very definite mark of appreciation be conveyed to this firm for the generous and wholehearted manner in which they have placed their knowledge at the disposal of the Americans. The officials of the production bureau were loud in their praise of the assistance they had received.

4. Such a combination did indeed take place in later years though not quite in the way that Johnson or Duke anticipated, much to the amusement of Henry Ford and the indignation of Rolls-Royce, neither of the firms being directly responsible.

CHAPTER 8

1. Of the three aero-engines which he had designed, the Falcon was undoubtedly Royce's favourite. He was not normally given to praising his own work, but in a memorandum on the subject of the Falcon written on 6 November 1917, he revealed his partiality for this engine.

   There are several reasons for believing that this is the very best engine of its horsepower in existence, and is preferred and demanded by the actual fighters at the front. This is of course a matter for the Air Board to decide, and for those interested to investigate. The probable reason why this engine is preferable to any other, in addition to its proved reliability and freedom from stoppages through breakages or wear, may be stated in a few words, that *having twelve cylinders properly arranged* * it has an excellent balance and very smooth turning moment, and therefore runs with less vibration than a six- or eight-cylinder engine which often has propeller troubles. It also has a reduction gear which is much more efficient than an ordinary spur gear and does not create high stresses within the gear chamber. The engine is light, but not extremely so, owing to the presence of all necessary adjuncts efficiently arranged, including a damped spring drive (Rolls-Royce patent) to all the secondary shafts, which avoids the inevitable high stresses created by the torsional deflection of the crankshaft. This, so far as we know, and the epicyclic reduction gear, are not yet fitted to any other aero engine known to us.

* The italics are mine. This was to become the classic V-12 liquid-cooled aero-engine type whose potentialities were not fully exhausted until the arrival of the gas-turbine. The design cannot really be said to have been superseded, since the gas-turbine employs an entirely different system of combustion. Royce's obvious confidence in this type is thus of unusual significance.

2. Basil Johnson had joined Rolls-Royce at his brother's invitation in March 1914, but he left the organisation when war broke out, and eventually became commanding officer of the Admiralty Stores Depot at the White City. He was released from this by the Admiralty at very short notice, and returned to Rolls-Royce at the Admiralty's request to take over his brother's work. Claude was able to spare him only a few hours to inform him of the state of the company's business before he left for America.

Index

Acton, Lord, 33
Admiralty, orders RR Eagles, 53; conflict with War Office, 53, 54; transfers responsibility for aero-engines to Ministry of Munitions, 63; offers encouragement to RR, 69; conference authorises new buildings, 73; orders more Eagles, 74; acts without Air Board approval, 75, 76; builds Hispano-Suiza factory, 77; releases engines to Sir Douglas Haig, 77; supports Department of Aeronautical Supplies, 78; develops Eagle production, 79; puts forward capital expenditure figures, 82; and Basil Johnson, 156
Aerial Operations Committee, General Smuts asked to chair, 89
Aeronautical Supplies, Department of, 78
Air Board (U.K.), established in 1916, 74; earns First Sea Lord's disapproval, 76; powers widened, 77; authority sought for repair shop, 79; agrees to concentrate on Eagle, 80; considers standardising RR output, 80; contemplates coercing RR to make agreement, 92; cables Johnson in U.S.A., 107; decides on major RR aero-engine programme, 118; meeting attended by Winston Churchill suggests new targets, 121; and meeting with U.S. Air Attachés, Appendix VII; and the Falcon engine, 156
Air Council, 130, 131
Air Ministry, historical records of, xxi; formation impeded by service departments, 76; recommended by General Smuts, 89; and post-war aero-engine requirements, 130, 131; and RR's reputation in 1918, 133
Air Policy Committee, Smuts becomes Chairman, 89
Air Production Board (U.S.), asks Nadin to inspect Saxon plant, 94; considers excess profits problem insoluble, 101; and advice given by Montgomery, 102; and Eagle production in U.S.A., 115,

142–6; and contract conditions, Appendix IV; and Pierce-Arrow negotiations, 146; and fall-back for Liberty failure, 155; view of RR generosity, 155
Air Raids, 88, 89
Aitken, Sir Maxwell (Lord Beaverbrook), makes bid to acquire control, 39; dissuaded from bid by Arthur Gibbs, 40; agrees to issue preference shares, 41; and Whitehall methods, 71; and Pierce-Arrow merger, 112
Alexander, General, 122, 129, 130
Allen & Co. Ltd, 65
Aluminium Casting Co. Inc., 116
Amalgamated Society of Engineers, 61
Andrews, P. W. S., and business history, xxiii; and cost curves, 151
Argyll Motor Co. Ltd, liquidated and re-organised, 15; new issue oversubscribed in 1905, 15; balance sheet considered by RR directors, 17; disappearance of £750,000, 41
Armistice (1918), 126
Armstrong-Siddeley Ltd, 133
Armstrong-Whitworth Ltd, 65; refuse to accept RR conditions, 69; continue negotiations, 73
Asquith, Mr, 62
Austin Motor Co., 78
Automobiles Rolls-Royce de France, launched in 1911, 37; considered for repair works and assembly plant, 38; accumulated losses, 42; costing £1000 a month, 54

Bailhache Committee, 68, 74
Baker, Newton D., 109, 110
Balfour, Mr Arthur, 76
Beaverbrook, Lord, see Aitken, Sir Maxwell
Belnap, L. J., xx
Benn, I. H., 39
Bentley engine, 78
B.H.P. engine, 78, 90
Blainey & Co. Inc., 93